ADULT WOMAN WITH ADHD

THE UNCONVENTIONAL GUIDE TO COPING WITH NEURODIVERSITY WITH TIPS FOR AVOIDING DISTRACTIONS, MANAGING EMOTIONS AND NO LONGER FEELINGLIKE A FAILURE, TURNING INTO A SUPERWOMAN.

By
Pansy Bradley

© **Copyright 2023. All Rights Reserved.**

The publication is sold with the idea that the publisher is not required to render accounting, officially permitted or otherwise qualified services. This document is geared towards providing exact and reliable information concerning the topic and issue covered. If advice is necessary, legal or professional, a practiced individual in the profession should be ordered.

- From a Declaration of Principles which was accepted and approved equally by a Committee of the American Bar Association and a Committee of Publishers and Associations.

In no way is it legal to reproduce, duplicate, or transmit any part of this document in either electronic means or printed format. Recording of this publication is strictly prohibited, and any storage of this document is not allowed unless with written permission from the publisher—all rights reserved.

The information provided herein is stated to be truthful and consistent. Any liability, in terms of inattention or otherwise, by any usage or abuse of any policies, processes, or directions contained within is the sole and utter responsibility of the recipient reader. Under no circumstances will any legal responsibility or blame be held against the publisher for any reparation, damages, or monetary loss due to the information herein, either directly or indirectly.

Respective authors own all copyrights not held by the publisher.

The information herein is offered for informational purposes solely and is universal as so. The presentation of the information is without a contract or any guarantee assurance.

The trademarks that are used are without any consent, and the publication of the trademark is without permission or backing by the trademark owner. All trademarks and brands within this book are for clarifying purposes only and are owned by the owners themselves, not affiliated with this document

Table of Content

- INTRODUCTION 4
- PART ONE: THE BASICS 5
  - UNDERSTANDING ADHD 6
  - WHAT ARE THE DIFFERENT TYPES OF ADHD 21
  - CAUSES AND SYMPTOMS OF ADHD 23
  - HOW TO DIAGNOSE ADHD 33
  - MYTH ABOUT ADHD 51
  - ADHD BRAIN VS. NORMAL BRAIN 60
  - CO-OCCURRING CONDITION IN ADHD 68
  - THE NEGATIVE EFFECT OF ADHD, IF NOT TREATED 75
- PART TWO: ADHD IN WOMEN 79
  - HOW TO KNOW IF A WOMAN HAS ADHD 80
  - IMPACT OF ADHD ON WOMEN 83
  - WHAT CAUSES ADHD IN WOMEN 86
  - RISK FACTORS FOR WOMEN WITH ADHD 90
  - HOW ADHD SYMPTOMS DIFFER IN WOMEN 93
  - WHY ADHD IS UNDERDIAGNOSED IN WOMEN 94
  - THE RIGHT DIAGNOSES FOR WOMEN WITH ADHD 97
  - THE GOOD SIDE OF ADHD IN WOMEN 106
  - HOW TO MANAGE EMOTIONS IN A WOMAN WITH ADHD 110
  - RIGHT NUTRITION FOR A WOMAN WITH ADHD 112
  - AN EFFECTIVE METHOD FOR COPING WITH ADHD 114
  - HOW TO TREAT ADHD IN WOMEN 116
  - HOW TO USE EXERCISE IN TREATING ADHD IN WOMEN 119
  - HOW TO USE MINDFULNESS FOR WOMEN WITH ADHD 126
  - HOW TO MANAGE THE RELATIONSHIP FOR WOMEN WITH ADHD 131
  - HOW TO MANAGE WORK FOR WOMEN WITH ADHD 138
  - HOW TO MANAGE MONEY FOR WOMEN WITH ADHD 140
  - HOW TO IMPROVE FOCUS IN WOMEN WITH ADHD 142
  - STIGMA IN WOMEN WITH ADHD 144
  - LIVING WITH A WOMAN DIAGNOSED WITH ADHD 148
  - LIFE MANAGEMENT TOOLS FOR WOMEN WITH ADHD 153
  - SELF-LOVE FOR WOMEN WITH ADHD 157
- CONCLUSION 161

INTRODUCTION

Millions of adults struggle with ADULT ATTENTION DEFICIT HYPERACTIVITY DISORDER (ADHD), a childhood disorder that can lead to memory, depression, attention, and other issues. Adult ADHD can affect people of any sex, but women are more likely to have it. Nearly 5 million American women are affected by this neurological condition, which has more severe effects on women than on males.

Many children with attention issues go on to have attention issues as adults. Adults may exhibit emotional reactivity, underperformance, low self-esteem, harmed relationships, or depression; disorganization is the most pervasive among them.

Disarray can grow to mythical proportions. Overflowing cabinets, stacks of items with baby piles, missed meetings, persistent delay, and confused thinking are all signs of disorganization and are all connected to an unreliable attention system. One woman claims she sits down since she has so much to do and is unsure where to begin.

Additionally, there is the irritation and guilt of finding what other people do to be so simple and difficult, as well as the sense of abandonment as friends and coworkers move on with their lives. At the same time, you seem stuck like Sisyphus, constantly arranging papers that inevitably fall into disarray. What are you doing these days? The others cease asking because "organizing" is the same answer every time.

Learn what makes your brain light up. What do you enjoy? Make a place in your schedule for things that you enjoy.

This book teaches you how to cope with and overcome neurodiversity. You will master practical tips for managing symptoms. You would no longer feel like a failure because you would be transformed into a superwoman.

Let's get started!

PART ONE: THE BASICS

One of the prevalent mental health conditions impacting children worldwide is attention-deficit hyperactivity disorder (ADHD). Although the illness usually manifests in childhood, people may also experience symptoms. Most kids with ADHD exhibit crippling characteristics like inattentiveness, hyperactivity, and impulsivity that interfere with their daily tasks at home or school.

In 2011, the CDCreported that over 11% of Americans between the ages of 4 and 17 had been given an ADHD diagnosis.

The latest research indicates that women with ADHD experience even more emotional upheaval than males, and women are likely as men to suffer from ADHD. Despite significant advancements in diagnosing and managing ADHD, some experts may believe that the condition mostly affects boys and men rather than girls and women. As a result, women with ADHD are less likely to receive the right therapy and are more likely to be undetected (or obtain a wrong diagnosis) than males.

According to Fred Reimherr, M.D., the primary author of a recent study that discovered that ADHD had a disproportionate effect on women, "ADHD is still thought to be a male condition." The women had a significantly higher history of being given emotional-based psychiatric diagnoses, such as anxiety or mood disorders. I believe that a doctor treating grownups frequently concentrates on those symptoms. The underlying ADHD in a woman with emotional symptoms may go unnoticed.

UNDERSTANDING ADHD

The topic has been hotly disputed as more children have received attention deficit hyperactivity disorder diagnoses during the past two decades. Some people assume those with ADHD are sluggish, ignorant, and weak-willed. However, the National Institutes of Health and the U.S. Department of Education have acknowledged ADHD as a scientifically based condition.

Although adult ADHD has been formally recognized since 1978, it is typically diagnosed in youngsters. This is evident, especially given that the majority of children with ADHD go on to develop the same illness as adults.

The symptoms of ADHD are present into adulthood for 30% to 70% of children with the illness. Numerous studies have consistently demonstrated that ADHD is inherited, and a family with multiple children is likely to discover more than one has ADHD.

Additionally, children who have been given an ADHD diagnosis are more likely to have at least one parent or another close member who also has the condition. If one twin has the condition, twins are even more likely to both develop it.

Additionally, adults who were not diagnosed as children may exhibit more pronounced symptoms, complicating their relationships or careers. Many adults don't know they have ADHD, which leaves them perplexed about why their aspirations keep eluding them.

The pattern of ADHD in adults differs slightly from that in youngsters. Adults may frequently be late for work or significant occasions. Even though adults are aware that their late is impeding their aspirations, they struggle to arrive on time.

Your child is often distracted while performing schoolwork or chores and frequently daydreams while at school. Perhaps they fidget all the time. You could be concerned about whether or not they have ADHD (ADHD); another possibility is attention deficit disorder (ADD).

IS THERE A DISTINCTION?

No longer. The term "attention-deficit/hyperactivity disorder," or ADHD, was used by medical professionals in 1994 to encompass all attention-deficit disorders, even those in which the affected person is not hyperactive. The term "inattentive type" has since replaced terms like "ADHD, hyperactive/impulsive type," or "ADHD, mixed type."

Depending on your child's precise symptoms and diagnosis, your family should decide which term to use. To ensure your child receives the proper diagnosis, it is crucial to speak with a skilled mental health professional.

THE DIFFERENCES BETWEEN ADD AND ADHD AND HOW TO TELL THEM APART

Many people are confused about ADD and ADHD, but understanding how the two disorders differ can help dispel common misconceptions about the two completely different disorders and what each one entails. While Attention Deficit Hyperactive Disorder (ADHD), the abbreviation for the more complex condition known as Attention Deficit Disorder (ADD), may have physiological roots, it has a wide range of effects on a person. These effects include increased activity and more impulsive decision-making on the part of the affected person.

The person watching the affected person with ADHD is aware of their hyperactivity. However, there are several subtypes to both ailments that characterize the issues of the disorders. For example, people with ADD often have diminished abilities of attention. Below are a few of these:

For instance, many readers will be able to recall the stereotype of a person living with ADD as a young kid who bounces off the walls and drives educators and caregivers crazy. Compared to the more complex condition of ADD, ADHD is easy to describe, making it easier to spot the stereotyping that goes along with it. It is known to cause disruptions in the classroom and other related setbacks in a group situation. The sad thing with ADD is that even when the illness is less obvious, it still has a lot of harmful side effects.

Untreated ADD can make a person appear unusually "spaced-out" or disoriented to others, even though this is not the case. One example is when an ADD-er stares out the window while nothing is obvious for others to look at! Because of this, ADD is a challenging disorder to diagnose. As a result, many potential patients may receive inadequate care for many years, earning the label of "not being all there."

The outcome of this delayed diagnosis and subsequent denial of ADD treatment may be a person's mind wandering, which is no less unsettling for someone with the disorder. In addition, it was previously believed that boys were the only ones who experienced ADHD, but specialists now say that girls can also experience the illness, which may last until they are in their middle years! One significant distinction is that girls with ADD appear to report the inattentive form of the disorder, which is why it is usually misinterpreted as depression. Inattentive ADD may cause less obvious problems for the person who has it, and since there is less disturbance to those around them, many ADD-ers may suffer in quiet, without treatment, for years at a time, which adds to their anguish.

This is also why an early, accurate diagnosis of both limiting disorders is crucial for effective treatment. Academic contexts are the best bet for focusing on the implications of either disorder; in this way, whether a child has ADD or AHDH, interrupted or incomplete schoolwork won't be a problem.

Furthermore, the prompt diagnosis will assist parents in keeping a close eye on children with academic, psychological, and general issues. There are many signs of ADD or ADHD that attentive parents can look out for and seek help with if their children exhibit these warning signs indicating either disorder to get the best scope of treatment from timely counseling and therapy. These signs can range from difficulties with peer socialization to issues with orderliness to an inability to sit still for brief periods or mood swings (quiet to talkative).

Thus, it can be inferred that for a child's overall wellness program to be successful, one must pay equal attention to the psychological and physical facets of the child's upkeep.

Millions of kids and teens are affected by Attention Deficit Hyperactivity Disorder (ADHD), a serious and treatable medical illness. It is neither an urban legend nor only a disciplinary issue.

It is the most frequently identified pediatric psychiatric disease affecting between 3 and 5% of children worldwide, with symptoms appearing before age seven. Boys are diagnosed with it twice as often as girls.

However, it is sometimes overdiagnosed (when the diagnosis doesn't satisfy all DSM-IV core criteria) to account for conduct issues or obnoxious behaviors displayed by allegedly "hyper" children. Additionally, rather than trying to change the child's conduct, parents and teachers look for an easier control method.

Some individuals dismiss the possibility of ADHD or ADD and dismiss symptomatic kids as misbehaving or having inadequate parental discipline.

Using stimulant medications on a prescription as a "control" doesn't assist; it obscures the recognition of ADHD as a legitimate illness.

Although there is no specific test to diagnose ADHD, a clinical diagnosis is feasible.

The neurodevelopmental disorder attention deficit hyperactivity disorder (ADHD) frequently manifests in childhood. The illness may make it difficult for sufferers to control impulsive behaviors and their inability to concentrate on tasks, goals, and activities.

The hyperactivity component of ADHD receives the most public attention, but it is the less severe of the two issues. Early statistical analyses found that boys were more frequently impacted than girls since early studies concentrated on disruptive behavior in schools.

As a result of more recent studies on attention issues, doctors now understand that attention deficit disorder more frequently afflicts girls and women. In addition, even when hyperactive, girls don't exhibit the same outward signs as guys do.

All the main medical organizations acknowledge attention-deficit hyperactivity disorder as a legitimate diagnosis that has to be treated. However, several people, including some medical professionals and therapists, disagree.

You can find dozens of articles claiming it is a "controversy" if you search for "Is ADHD fake?" or "ADHD critics." Books and articles from the major media are among them.

Some claim that the method of diagnosis is the root of the issue. Critics contest a large number of ADHD patients.

According to Marilyn Wedge, Ph.D., author of A Disease Called Childhood, "you don't see children labeled with ADHD anywhere near the rate that American kids are."

It's accurate to say that the number of diagnoses has increased recently. This isrelated to the fact that more people are aware that in 2013, the guidelines used by medical practitioners to identify the illness altered.

According to Dr. Richard Saul, "kids are frequently misdiagnosed," which is another problem. He is the author of ADHD Does Not Exist. The signs of ADHD are undeniably real, according to Saul. But he adds, "there are a lot of diseases and health issues that can [create] those symptoms."

According to Saul, common conditions that might lead to hyperactivity and attention challenges include sleep disorders, depression, and issues with hearing and vision.

A doctor or therapist takes into account your medical history, the symptoms you report to them, any symptoms they may observe while watching you, and the opinions of other people who are familiar with you well (typically your family and your child's teachers). They may rate the frequency and severity of various behaviors using the "Conners' Teacher Rating Scale" or the "Vanderbilt questionnaire," such as:

- When explicitly addressed, she doesn't appear to be listening.
- has difficulty planning activities and tasks
- and difficulty waiting in line

A doctor or therapist "may make a mistake, especially if he or she doesn't have extensive experience with ADHD," advises Imad Alsakaf, MD, an assistant professor of psychiatry at Creighton University in Omaha, NE.

The illness is more frequently seen in patients who concurrently suffer from depression or substance addiction. According to psychologist Phil Glickman, PsyD, "These problems can disguise ADHD and make it harder to acquire the appropriate diagnosis."

Saul advises going to the doctor for a thorough physical examination and medical history. He also advises consulting a psychologist, and they have the time to conduct an in-depth evaluation, he claims.

The NEBA medical device, which analyzes brainwaves to assist clinicians in determining if ADHD or another ailment may cause a child's symptoms, received FDA approval in 2013. According to research, it should be used along with conventional diagnostic techniques.

Doctors are still learning about how the brain processes ADHD. MRIs, however, "reveal there are clear disparities between persons who have it and people who don't," according to Alsakaf.

He gestures toward the prefrontal cortex, a region of the brain that affects emotions, behavior, and problem-solving. Its activity is different in those with ADHD than those without it; however, these variations are insufficient to identify the illness.

Some professionals use the effectiveness of treatment as proof that the condition exists. When working with individuals with ADHD or parents of kids with ADHD who are skeptics, Glickman says, "I inform them that evidence from thousands of patients shows that behavioral therapies like talk therapy and medication improve ADHD symptoms."

Taking medicine and receiving counseling are frequent components of treatment. Some teenagers and adults who don't have the illness use some of these substances to increase their focus because they can be stimulating.

To obtain a prescription for habit-forming drugs, people who assert that they have ADHD symptoms are seen by doctors, according to Alsakaf. But that's not always the case.

You can seek a second opinion from a specialist qualified to assist with diagnosis and therapy, such as a psychiatrist or psychologist.

Alsakaf explains that the doctor "can communicate to you how ADHD works in a way that is relatable to you and help discover a treatment strategy that works." And that can significantly raise your standard of living.

If it turns out to be ADHD, Wedge advises non-medication therapy options, including regular exercise, screen time restrictions (particularly for "fast-paced" media like video games), and self-control training to help kids stay calm and perform well in and out of the classroom.

Do not immediately assume you have ADHD if you experience frequent restlessness and difficulty focusing. Other illnesses also frequently exhibit the same symptoms. A common indicator of depression is poor concentration, and restlessness or anxiety may indicate an overactive thyroid or an anxiety disorder. Your doctor will look into whether these issues could be contributing to your symptoms in addition to or instead of ADHD.

The conventional medical community has a simple, frequently narrow perspective on ADHD and its causes. Because of this, parents whose kids have recently received a diagnosis are given a brief explanation of ADHD, its signs, and why medication is the best course of action. Even though doctors mean well when they tell you this, their knowledge of this illness does not provide a comprehensive picture.

Here are four things every woman should know about ADHD.

NUMEROUS FACTORS CONTRIBUTE TO ADHD.

You may be aware that a lack of the brain chemicals dopamine and norepinephrine causes ADHD. While this is true, other factors contribute to the development of ADHD, and numerous factors might result in excessive hyperactivity and inattention.

In early childhood, exposure to neurotoxins can result in significant developmental delays.

A specific number of nutrients are required for the brain to function properly. Key vitamins, minerals, and nutrients can affect how neurotransmitters are produced, affecting ADHD symptoms.

A difficult birth might cause injury to the spine and the sensitive upper neck vertebrae, which can lead to ADHD.

Various foods and substances can cause allergic reactions, which might lead to undesirable behavior.

For this reason, a youngster is advised to undergo a rigorous testing process before receiving treatment.

ADHD HAS SYMPTOMS THAT OTHER DISEASES ALSO HAVE.

Inattention, impulsivity, and hyperactivity are not the only symptoms of ADHD. From autism to inner ear issues, many conditions exhibit the same symptoms. This is why a doctor should take the time to rule out associated conditions before prescribing a course of treatment rather than simply diagnosing a child after ticking off a list of symptoms.

YOU CANNOT OUTGROW ADHD.

One of the most pervasive misconceptions regarding ADHD is that it is a problem of childhood that most people overcome by the time they are teenagers or young adults. There is nothing more untrue. When untreated or without appropriate attention paid to the symptoms, ADHD frequently satisfies the diagnostic standards of associated disorders. An overactive child may grow up to exhibit antisocial conduct. Or perhaps a meek, unfocused teen lady will develop sadness. Once ADHD has been diagnosed, it's critical to find a therapy, but it's equally crucial to find one that addresses more than just the symptoms.

AS A GIFT, ADHD

The stereotypical image of an ADHD child is an annoying young boy who speaks excessively and cannot remain still for more than five seconds. While many ADHD kids exhibit undesirable behaviors, not all aspects of this disease are negative. According to studies, kids with ADHD think more creatively than kids without. The issue is that their illnesses hinder them from using these abilities in their social interactions and academic work. A child can eliminate the disorder's negative symptoms with the correct treatment plan while retaining its distinctive traits.

MEDICAL REALITY OR CONVENIENT JUSTIFICATION FOR HYPERACTIVITY?

Attention-Deficit Hyperactivity Disorder has generated more controversy than any other psychiatric diagnosis (ADHD). Some detractors claim that the diagnosis of "ADHD" is simply a pretext used by angry parents and overzealous medical professionals to "medicate away" a child's bothersome behaviors. While some detractors acknowledge the existence of ADHD, many feel it is significantly over-diagnosed.

These assertions occasionally hold some validity, but there are now compelling clinical and academic studies demonstrating that ADHD is a real condition with a strong biological basis and that, if anything, it is frequently underdiagnosed.

Contrary to widespread belief, no conclusive evidence exists that an excessively sugary diet causes ADHD. Furthermore, research over the past 20 years has shown that ADHD in children is not necessarily "outgrown." Depending on whether we count only the full-blown disease or even just a few ADHD symptoms, between 4% and 30% of ADHD children will exhibit symptoms in adulthood.

WHAT DOES CHILDHOOD ADHD RESEMBLE?

Take Shawn, an 11-year-old who spent more than five years as a "problem kid." Shawn had problems staying still in class starting at age 5. After only a half-hour of class, Shawn would fidget, wriggle in his seat, or even get up and leave. Despite repeated warnings to sit down by the teacher, he occasionally ran about the classroom. Shawn struggled to pay attention in class and frequently appeared to be "off in a cloud." He hardly ever completed his chores, duties, or homework assignments for school or the house. Shawn could not complete any activity that required more than a few minutes of steady focus. He struggled to remember basic instructions and was easily distracted by the smallest noise. Sometimes Shawn would sputter replies before the inquiry was finished, and he found it difficult to wait in line. Shawn occasionally interfered with other kids' games by clamoring to be allowed to join them.

Even though the youngster in this image appears to have ADHD pretty frequently, this disorder can manifest in numerous ways. Although several studies indicate that boys are more likely than girls to have ADHD, this may be because parents and instructors tend to find girls to be less disruptive than boys, which results in fewer complaints.

Therefore, despite their conduct appearing normal on the outside, girls with significant attentional issues may have ADHD.

Of course, additional issues such as boredom, subpar instruction, and despair might impair a child's attention span. This is why a pediatrician or mental health specialist must thoroughly evaluate the child to diagnose ADHD in children. Untreated ADHD in adulthood may manifest as a "personality disorder," alcoholism, agitation, or antisocial behavior.

People are frequently diagnosed with ADHD when young, but its consequences can last into adulthood. Boys are more frequently diagnosed with ADHD, while many girls and women are underdiagnosed.

WHAT DISTINGUISHES GIRLS FROM BOYS?
Girls who exhibit attention deficit disorder with or without hyperactivity typically fall into one of four categories, none of which are as loud and disruptive as the boys.

1. Although Julia enjoys running around, climbing trees, and playing with her brothers, she is often peaceful at home and strives to please her father. Her nickname is **"Tomboy"** by some. She makes an effort, despite being sloppy and frequently lacking in completion, and her substandard academic performance is regarded as the most she is capable of.
2. When Donna's instructor calls on her, she smiles nicely and makes a tremendous effort to follow instructions despite sitting at the back of the classroom and frequently looking out the window. She sometimes gives the impression that she is paying attention when completely lost. She works more slowly than the other students in her class and frequently drops the ball on finishing tasks. However, no one knows she is struggling because she is helpful and kind. She is "spacey" or "dreamy" by nature.
3. Susan chatters on and on while laughing, frequently considering her upcoming activities or a weekend party. She often jumps around from the beginning of an event to the end and back again when describing it. She is entertaining to be around because she is bursting with ideas and excitement, but she becomes very upset when someone disagrees with

her. She can seem "silly" to hide her disarray and forgetfulness. She is also very talkative and emotional. As she ages, her excessive energy may cause her to experiment dangerously with drugs, cigarettes, or sexual activities to make up for her subpar academic performance.
4. Deborah performed remarkably well in school, earning a Ph.D. and a top-notch career. Although she had worked considerably harder than her contemporaries to succeed academically, her attention issues did not truly surface until she married and had kids. Then, a significant depression resulted from the extreme complexity of life with employment, a husband, and children.

Girls are typically better behaved, so they do not draw attention, whereas hyperactive boys are likely to receive the care they need since they are disruptive. When they do receive attention, it is less likely to be directed at their attention issues than at character issues, such as the fact that Julia is not ladylike, Susan is a social butterfly rather than an academic, Donna is a little slow, and Deborah has a hint of the baby blues. ADHD is not often thought of.

Social expectations placed on women with ADHD in their feminine roles as wives and mothers—roles that call for a high level of organization—put them at a double disadvantage.

Think about what attention deficiency implies for a second. You're probably familiar with dimmers, those gadgets that let you change the brightness of a lamp for a romantic evening or a focused work session. Like a lamp, a brain requires an electric current to operate. Dopamine usage in the synapse is inefficient in ADD brains, acting as a dimmer. Since the current flowing through ADD brains is insufficient, stimulation is necessary to boost output. Risk and novelty are two ways ADD people can become awake.

Let's go back to our housewife, who has the same thousand daily tasks, including the same dishes to put in the dishwasher and remove, the same filthy socks to gather, wash, pair, and store, the same shirts to iron, etc. It's all tedious. There are also the children to dress, feed, get ready, transport to the doctor or tennis lessons, and plan social events.

Once more, the word "arrange" is included. The ADD brain operates with the dimmer on minimum, making decisions on what to do first, what is most important, or remembering to pick up the dry cleaning.

Susan, who ran away from school as quickly as possible, felt inadequate as a homemaker.

Workplace life might or might not be friendlier, and a PhD-holding woman like Deborah might flourish in a position that tests her skills and capitalizes on her interests. However, women who struggle in school, like Julia or Donna, are more likely to pursue low-level professions like housework that require the precise abilities they lack, like filing, neatly accurate typing, or recalling diners' orders.

The workplace frequently necessitates a lot of socializing, which may be challenging for someone like Donna, who prefers to keep to herself, or even Susan, the socialite who tends to be emotional, or Julia, with her "Tomboy" attitude who can find herself rejected by both men and women. Deborah might even be "too" smart.

WHY DOES ADHD OCCUR?

Neurotransmitters control attention and are less active in brain regions in patients with ADHD. The source of this chemical imbalance is unknown, but because ADHD frequently runs in families, researchers believe genes may be involved. Additionally, studies have connected prenatal alcohol and cigarette exposure to ADHD.

The world's nomadic peoples are more likely to have one genetic variant that results in symptoms resembling ADHD. Researchers believe that characteristics like impulsiveness, novelty seeking, and unpredictable behavior may aid nomads in finding food and other resources. Therefore, the same traits that make it difficult to succeed at a desk job may have worked to our ancestors' advantage when they lived as nomads.

FACTORS THAT INCREASE ADULT ADHD

1. INADEQUATE EXERCISE

Your ADHD may be the cause of your fuzzy memory. Additionally, not getting enough exercise is not good for your brain. However, exercise might enhance your memory. You can study, pay attention, and make decisions with its assistance. It's time to freshen up those sneakers!

2. FREQUENT EATING OUT

Even though preparing dinner isn't particularly difficult, people living with ADHD must put in a lot of extra mental effort. You must prepare, plan, and follow instructions. Yes, going out is simpler, but you should only do it seldom. You can treat ADHD with healthy eating, but it's difficult to eat well while traveling. Food from restaurants is a calorie, sugar, salt, and fat-dense. Additionally, you won't consume enough fruits and vegetables.

3. A SURPLUS OF JUNK FOOD

Science hasn't yet determined which foods, if any, exacerbate ADHD. However, evidence suggests that extraneous items, such as food coloring, may exacerbate certain children's symptoms. These ingredients can be found in processed meals like soda and confectionery. Scientists are unsure if it impacts adults, but cutting out junk food can't hurt. Check it out and see if it helps your issues.

4. SKIPPING BREAKFAST

Your symptoms can worsen if you skip that breakfast. Having breakfast can help you deal with social settings more easily. Early in the day, it can also improve your thinking and prolong your period of concentration. Try to eat something, even if your medications make you feel apathetic toward food. You can also use a container of yogurt or a hard-boiled egg.

5. MESSY OFFICES AND HOMES

Clutter, according to some, is a sign of greatness. According to research, it might imply creativity. However, a disorganized nest may exacerbate some symptoms. You are reminded of all the tasks you must complete by the heaps of papers, books, or clothes, and it could be too much at times. On the other hand, getting rid of the clutter might increase your productivity and reduce your anxiety.

6. TOO MUCH MATERIAL

While constant shopping might be enjoyable, it can also result in hoarding. You can find it simple to accumulate too much stuff and difficult to let it go if you have ADHD. The good news is that you can keep your cool when shopping. Adhere to the "one in, one out" principle. You must give away an old object before bringing in a new one.

7. WRONG MEDICINES

Were you truthful about your life and symptoms when your doctor diagnosed you with ADHD? If not, you can receive the incorrect treatment and end up worse. Why?

If you have issues with substance misuse, ADHD medications may not always be effective.

Drugs used to treat serious depression can exacerbate ADHD. Some ADHD drugs may exacerbate anxiety.

8. SLEEP DEPRIVATION

Sleep issues and ADHD frequently coexist. Some people's cause is a stimulant drug. Others attribute their symptoms to disorders associated with ADHD, such as anxiety, sadness, and others. You're not only tired if you don't get enough sleep. Additionally, it can make symptoms like difficulty focusing and poor motor skills worse. Your physician can assist. Inform them of the situation.

9. GIVING UP THERAPY

Keep taking treatment and medicine if you're feeling better. Once you believe your ADHD is under control, you might be inclined to stop therapy. After all, taking a drug simplifies things, and counseling is expensive. However, evidence indicates that it significantly improves ADHD symptoms, particularly with medications. If you skip it, your symptoms can get worse.

10. SCREEN TIME ABUSE

Could your technology be exacerbating your symptoms? Maybe. Doctors have discovered connections between excessive screen time and ADHD. ADHD symptoms might potentially become more severe as a result of internet addiction. We're not yet sure which issue feeds the other, though. What is known is that using a screen right before bed can interfere with your sleep, which will exacerbate the symptoms of ADHD.

11. LACK OF CAFFEINE

Your coffee or tea habit might help with your ADHD symptoms. It follows that quitting the habit can make you feel worse. Tea contains caffeine, which may increase alertness, improve attention, and enhance brain function. Additionally, it might improve your working memory. Enjoy caffeine if your doctor says it's okay to do so!

SIGNIFICANT NEW STUDIES TO KNOW

Nearly 4 million children in the United States are affected by ADHD, also known as Attention Deficit Hyperactivity Disorder. It was originally identified over a century ago and made its sufferers abnormally hyperactive, inattentive, or impulsive.

Symptoms often start before age seven and manifest as an inability to operate regularly at work, among friends, at home, and in the case of adults, at school. The challenge is that we are unable to pinpoint this illness precisely. However, studies indicate that it is related to unequal brain development, namely lower brain sizes and poor frontal and right brain functioning. Some patients catch up in growth and recover from the illness.

The prefrontal cortical circuits in the front brain, or the ADHD brain, need the proper amount of catecholamine transmission, which is associated with ADHD, at least in some circumstances, according to recent studies. Medical stimulants like methylphenidate and more recent non-stimulant medications are the most often used therapies for ADHD. These medications all work by enhancing catecholamine transmission in the frontal lobes.

Another study with potentially harmful implications links mental disorders like ADHD to an increased likelihood of developing alcohol use issues. It took eight years for Dr. Nora Volkow of the NIDA (National Institute on Drug Abuse) to conduct the study with the assistance of other researchers, some of whom were from the Mount Sinai Medical Center.

Following an injection of a substance that demonstrates how dopamine interacts with brain receptors, Volkow's team used PET scans to examine precise images of the brain. It was shown that patients with ADHD possessed significantly fewer mid-brain regions that comprise the "reward pathway," which links inputs to pleasant expectations. This study forewarns us about the mental therapies required to prevent drinking and drug abuse in those with ADHD, especially in young people.

Although these medications are used extensively to treat ADHD, there are considerable worries regarding their unknowable long-term effects. As a result, parents and physicians are in a difficult position and must carefully weigh the alleged advantages of utilizing these medications against their unknown side effects.

Adults with the illness exhibit significant procrastination, disorganization, difficulty meeting deadlines, and impulsivity that is out of the ordinary. Many people live their entire lives with undiagnosed symptoms.

The truth is that there are numerous myths surrounding ADHD, and they are more harmful than helpful. Despite suggestions that it is a problem with willpower, it is a chemical imbalance in the brain.

WHAT ARE THE DIFFERENT TYPES OF ADHD

There is no one-size-fits-all diagnosis or course of treatment for ADHD. Everyone is unique.

The American Psychiatric Association has recognized three types. Each has unique symptoms, and each is treated according to those symptoms.

Three types of symptoms are frequently present in people with ADHD.

1. INATTENTIVE ADHD

This disorder doesn't cause hyperactivity in children, and they lack the excessive energy characteristic of people with ADHD. Children of this kind may appear bashful or "in their world."

A youngster under 16 is considered to have ADD if they exhibit 6 or more symptoms of inattention (5 or more for older teens) for at least six months in a row without exhibiting any signs of hyperactivity or impulsivity.

These are the symptoms of inattentive ADHD:
- having trouble concentrating
- being prone to distraction and frequently making BLUNDERS
- frequently missing essential stuff
- neglecting to pay attention to details
- committing thoughtless errors
- Inability to follow or understand instructions
- Failure to pay attention and stay on the job
- avoiding difficult chores and getting sidetracked
- being absentminded
- losing items that are needed to finish missions
- dislikes or avoids demanding mental effort (such as homework)
- Problems focusing in class, at home, or even when playing.
- Disorganized and appear forgetful
- When addressed directly, she doesn't seem to be listening, doesn't pay close attention to details

As a result of the symptoms, perhaps being mistaken for daydreaming, children with this subtype of ADHD may go undetected.

2. IMPULSIVE-HYPERACTIVE TYPE

Children with this type of ADHD are energetic and continually move in problematic ways. If a child under 16 exhibits six or more hyperactive/impulsive symptoms for at least six months, it is diagnosed (5 or more for older teens). Compared to the unfocused form, this one is more observable.

There are several ways that impulsivity and hyperactivity manifest. These signs include:

- Answering questions quickly before they're finished.
- Interrupting other people frequently
- difficulty holding out for their turn
- talks too much
- Tapping, wriggling, and fidgeting
- when it's not proper, gets up (such as when the teacher is talking or in the middle of dinner)
- Running or climbing in the wrong places
- Can't play quietly
- restlessness
- excessive chatting and frequent disruptions during conversations combined with problems staying sitting
- frequent standing while seated
- When not acceptable, engage in running or climbing
- Talking excessively, interrupting others, or blabbing
- Frequently in motion, as if "powered by a motor."

3. COMBINED TYPE

The most typical form of ADHD is this one. Always "on the Go." Both hyperactive-impulsive and inattentive symptoms are present in those who have it.

Both inattentive and hyperactive-impulsive symptoms characterize ADHD with mixed symptoms.

According to a 2019 study, girls may not receive the proper treatment for their ADHD since they frequently exhibit more signs of inattentive ADHD than hyperactive-impulsive ADHD.

Parents, schools, and healthcare professionals are less likely to notice the relatively quiet distractibility of inattentive ADHD because the symptoms of hyperactive-impulsive ADHD can be louder and more disruptive.

CAUSES AND SYMPTOMS OF ADHD

With more and more children falling prey to ADHD, it has become extremely important to throw light on the topic and spread awareness. Sadly, many parents are still uninformed about the exact ADHD symptoms, so the children are not treated properly. Timely detection and subsequent therapy can go a long way in curing ADHD. Here are some of the most common ADHD symptoms.

HYPERACTIVITY:
Hyperactivity is a very common ADHD symptom. Suppose you notice your child is finding it difficult to sit in one place, is very fidgety, keeps moving around, or constantly talks even while engaged in a task, in all likelihood. In that case, they are affected by attention deficit hyperactivity disorder.

INATTENTIVENESS:
Inattentiveness is another major indicator of ADHD. Children who are unable to pin their attention on a single activity, get bored quickly, or are almost always distracted - can be affected by attention deficit hyperactivity disorder. They even find it difficult to concentrate, are always lost in their world (daydreaming about improbable things), and can seldom follow instructions.

IMPULSIVENESS:
Children exhibiting this symptom are also most likely to be diagnosed with ADHD. A child with impulsiveness usually cannot wait for their turn at a game/recital and is not worried about the consequences of an inappropriate action. They also make improper and uncalled-for comments at the wrong moments. This happens because the child is not in control of their emotions.

These are the most common symptoms of ADHD. In some cases, the symptoms are very clearly visible; in others, they can be far less pronounced. The symptoms can be separated or clubbed together. Of the three listed symptoms, hyperactivity and impulsiveness are usually easy to detect. However, inattentiveness as a symptom can be a little confusing to detect. The child usually sits down, interacts well with peers, and doesn't show many behavioral problems.

While looking to identify the symptoms of attention deficit hyperactivity disorder, the following should be remembered:

1. The child must exhibit the symptoms for at least six months before ADHD can be determined.
2. Every child suffering from hyperactivity, inattentiveness, and impulsiveness isn't affected by ADHD. However, these should never be ignored. A check-up can easily detect the disorder and help in the recovery process.
3. Children with impulsiveness symptoms can be mistaken as having emotional problems. This is not true in most cases, and as mentioned above, the slightest doubt must be cleared, as early detection can go a long way in curing the child completely.

Healthy and safe treatment is essential for a child with ADHD, as harmful chemical drugs can severely damage the bodily activities of the child. So once the symptoms have been identified, ensure you take your child to a therapist who gently addresses the problem. Alternative medication like homeopathy is also gaining a lot of popularity. Check out the various options available and help your child recover completely and healthily.

ADHD is characterized by difficulties focusing on the work at hand. When kids and adults operate a vehicle, that might lead to issues. According to studies, drivers who have ADHD are more likely to speed, cause accidents, and lose their licenses.

Adults with ADHD may struggle to prioritize, begin, and complete tasks. They frequently exhibit disarray and agitation and are quickly distracted. Some persons with ADHD find it difficult to focus while reading. Careers, goals, and relationships can all be derailed by an inability to maintain concentration and finish tasks.

Adults with ADHD may struggle with maintaining self-control. This may result in the following:
- Struggling to restrain my fury
- Impetuous actions
- blurting forth offensive or unpleasant ideas

Some persons with ADHD can hyperfocus on activities they find engaging or interesting. But they find it difficult to focus on boring jobs. The problem is that many routine tasks, like preparing a grocery list or submitting paperwork at work, are crucial for success in daily living. People with ADHD frequently put off tedious duties in favor of more pleasurable pursuits.

These days, it could appear like everyone has ADHD because of how quickly we respond to texts, emails, calls, and hectic work situations. Although this can be distracting, most people can concentrate on their most pressing obligations, and distractions prevent people with ADHD from finishing important tasks at work and home.

Poor handwriting has been linked to several theories, including language difficulties, mechanical writing difficulties, genetic variables, and other hand-eye coordination and motor control issues that can be present in children with ADHD.

ADHD is a mental illness that impairs one's capacity to do any or all of the following tasks:

- long-term paying attention, focusing, or concentration
- taking note of certain information and dividing tasks and objectives into phases or steps
- maintaining order and controlling timetables
- recalling information while seated, controlling impulses

From person to person, ADHD might look different. It can be a good idea to discuss your symptoms with a healthcare provider if you can relate to many of them. For examples:

- I often feel as though I have no control over my life.
- I don't normally invite people over because my house is always messy.
- I try to hide the reality that I feel completely out of place and behind at school and work.
- Even when I recall appointments, I frequently arrive late.
- I repeatedly read the same phrase. Even when something is significant, it takes me a long time to read.
- In lengthy meetings, I grow restless and fidgety. I find meetings to be almost usually excessively lengthy.
- I wish I could cut out all the interruptions. Similarly, blurting.
- I waste time looking for things I've misplaced or lost.
- I've been involved in more car accidents than I should have.
- I have a lot of paper in my life, including bills I forgot to pay and reminders for critical tasks like renewing my driver's license.
- People have occasionally said that I don't seem to be listening to them.
- I always freeze or put off starting a huge job because I have no idea where to begin.
- I act impulsively to escape from or forget when things seem too out of control. I might overspend, overeat, or drink excessively.

- I tend to concentrate excessively on one task while neglecting others.
- Although I'm incredibly skilled at making objectives, I frequently give up on them or become sidetracked before finishing them.
- Due to my inability to maintain organization and follow through, I have lost employment.
- For the same reasons, I've experienced relationship issues.
- I feel anxious and depressed about it all.

Children with ADHD exhibit typical behavior in a much more extreme and intense way than other kids. While running around and playing loudly is normal for kids, sometimes, an ADHD child will do so excessively and when it is not suitable. A child without the condition can be boisterous in the schoolyard yet quiet and focused in a learning environment. Even though they are supposed to be attentive and non-disruptive, children with ADHD continue to act out.

The majority of kids with ADHD still do as teenagers. The signs of ADHD in teenagers are comparable to those in kids. They consist of the following:
- Distractibility
- Disorganization
- inadequate focus
- Hyperactivity
- Impulsivity

ADHD symptoms may worsen during the adolescent years, particularly as the hormonal changes of puberty continue and the demands of high school and extracurricular activities rise.

Many teenagers with ADHD struggle in school due to attention issues and poor focus. Grades may decline, particularly if the teenager is not receiving treatment for ADHD.

Teens with ADHD frequently miss homework, misplace textbooks, and get bored with everyday schoolwork. Teenagers may become impulsive or too attentive, not waiting for their turn to speak before responding. They might talk over students and teachers and speed through homework. Teens with ADHD may also be restless and find it difficult to concentrate in class.

Teens with ADHD are frequently too preoccupied with concentrating on other things to remember the work. This is particularly evident concerning homework, physical prowess, and peer connections. Due to their lack of focus, individuals frequently receive poor test results and are rejected from peer groups, sports teams, and after-school activities.

HOW SEX AFFECTS THE SIGNS OF ADHD
The signs of ADHD can differ from individual to person. It's not always possible to ensure that each person receives the proper treatment by making generalizations based on sex or gender.
Here are the results of recent studies on gender differences in ADHD symptoms.

HORMONES AND ADHD
Changes in hormone levels can affect ADHD symptoms in both sexes. Individuals may suffer a change in symptoms around puberty when sex hormones affect physical symptoms and behavior, regardless of the sex assigned to them at birth. Other ways that fluctuating hormones can impact symptoms include:
- Hormone levels during menopause and pregnancy can also exacerbate symptoms.
- An increase follows the ovulation period of your menstrual cycle in inattention.
- A woman with ADHD who may exhibit greater impulsivity may see an increase in ADHD symptoms due to changes in estrogen levels throughout her cycle.

ADHD'S NEGATIVE PSYCHOLOGICAL AND EMOTIONAL IMPACT ON WOMEN
Girls with ADHD frequently have poorer self-esteem than boys with ADHD, even far into adulthood. Girls with ADHD frequently engage in more conflict in their social connections than girls without ADHD. Women and girls with ADHD are likelier to have eating disorders, anxiety, and sadness symptoms. Additionally, women who have been previously or concurrently diagnosed with the hyperactive-impulsive form of ADHD are more likely to report having a borderline personality disorder.

IS ADHD TO BLAME FOR YOUR SEXUAL ISSUES?
According to research, 40% of men and women with ADHD will experience some sexual difficulties. However, there are many things you may do to deal with your problems.

SEXUAL PROBLEMS AND ADHD
People with ADHD sometimes experience certain common sex problems. They consist of the following:

DIFFICULTY FOCUSING DURING INTIMATE MOMENTS.
One of the most well-known signs of ADHD is difficulty focusing. As a result, you might discover that your thoughts wander while you're hugging, having sex, or engaging in foreplay. They might assume you're not interested in them if you're with a partner. And occasionally, that lack of concentration can make it more difficult to experience orgasm.

A STRONG OR WEAK LIBIDO.
You might have a high sex drive if you have ADHD. You could regularly consider having sex or attempting to do so, and you might frequently watch porn. On the other hand, a decreased sex drive can be brought on by some ADHD drugs. Your libido is most likely to decline if you use antidepressants, which are occasionally used to treat ADHD.

UNEXPECTED SHIFTS IN YOUR EMOTIONS OR DESIRES.
People with ADHD frequently experience mood swings. Hypersensitivity is another characteristic of this illness, implying that for someone with ADHD, experiences like touch that may feel normal to someone else may be excessively strong.
Your sex desire and how you connect with romantic relationships may be affected by hypersensitivity and mood swings. For instance, you might have formerly enjoyed a particular sex act before deciding you no longer do. Alternatively, you might enjoy touching or snuggling one day but not the next. Additionally, sex actions that may be pleasurable for your spouse may irritate or unnerve you.

A SEXUALLY DANGEROUS BEHAVIOR IS DESIRED
Lower neurotransmitters, brain chemicals, are frequently found in people with ADHD. You may be more likely to act impulsively and take risks, such as engaging in unprotected sex, if your neurotransmitter levels are low. ADHD does not always result in dangerous conduct. But it's crucial to understand that you might eventually wish to engage in sexual actions that aren't necessarily safe or healthy.

You become less interested in sex or romantic relationships due to anger and loneliness. You might feel furious or lonely if you have ADHD, and these feelings could be exhausting and decrease your desire for sex.

Relationship problems brought on by ADHD symptoms might make it more difficult for you and your spouse to enjoy intimacy. For instance, mood swings may increase your propensity for conflict. You might also fall asleep during chats or heated exchanges, giving the impression that you are disregarding your companion.

STEPS TO TAKE

You can control your ADHD symptoms in several ways, and this may increase your chances of engaging in fulfilling love and sexual interactions.

Administer your medication as directed. The majority of ADHD drugs won't impair your sex desire. The exact reverse is true: They make it easier for you to concentrate, which can make it easier for you to enjoy sex. Additionally, these medications aid in limiting dangerous conduct, which can support your overall health. Some people with ADHD find that keeping their focus during intimacy is aided by having sex closer to the time they take their medication.

Discuss your medicine with your doctor. Inform your doctor or pharmacist if you do experience sexual problems and believe that your medications are to blame. They might be able to assist you in making adjustments that will improve your mood. For instance, changing antidepressants could increase a person's low sex drive.

Exercise. Being active can improve focus and neurotransmitter levels, increasing your enjoyment of intimacy and decreasing your propensity to participate in dangerous sexual conduct.

Share your symptoms with your companion. Inform your spouse that ADHD symptoms, such as difficulty focusing, can manifest themselves during sex. Your spouse must understand that this doesn't mean you're not interested in them.

Think about speech therapy. According to research, talk therapy, commonly referred to as psychotherapy, can lessen the effects of ADHD on your sex life. A therapist can also assist you in acquiring knowledge that will improve your ability to converse with your partner, both in and out of bed.

During sex, speak up. Tell your spouse how you want to be touched and if you don't feel like getting close. Speaking your truth can help you avoid conflicts and other communication problems.

Minimize distractions. Have intercourse in a dimly lit or darkened environment if you tend to get distracted during sexual activity. It might assist you in maintaining the presence of your partner.

CAUSES OF ADHD- PARENTS, AND FAMILIES
The believe that parents are to blame for their children's bad behavior is the most difficult to debunk of all the misconceptions and public views ADHD produces. It has been suggested that parenting approaches (such as being overly critical), the home environment, lifestyles, and even prenatal issues might exacerbate symptoms or increase a child's likelihood of developing ADHD. Let's disentangle fact from fantasy to explore this myth.

ADHD HAS A HEREDITARY FOUNDATION.
Parents are indirectly to blame for their child's ADHD. Numerous studies have linked heredity to ADHD; in fact, most medical professionals think that genetics alone is the only source of the disorder. According to studies, children are more likely to experience ADHD if one or both of their parents do as well. Twin studies, which show that identical twins are more likely to share the illness than fraternal twins, even if they were raised in different homes, have proven the genetic foundation for the disorder. The existence of an "ADHD gene" cannot be detected by tests, and it is not much you can do to influence the genes your child inherits. By avoiding the environmental elements that are known to cause ADHD, you can, nevertheless, reduce your risk of developing the condition.

SOME DOMESTIC SITUATIONS CAUSE ADHD
A child's genetic susceptibility to ADHD does not guarantee that the disorder will manifest. Only certain environmental triggers cause ADHD, including the child's eating habits and lifestyle choices. However, suffice it to say that a diet high in processed carbs, food additives, and empty calories exacerbates any nutrient deficiencies or food intolerances a child with ADHD may already have.

We have articles that go into great length about these environmental factors. ADHD symptoms can also be attributed to a sedentary lifestyle that includes video games and other similar activities. Instead of using medication to treat ADHD, parents should develop a thorough treatment plan for their child that includes plenty of physical activity and a balanced diet.

Children exposed to alcohol and cigarette smoke during pregnancy and childbirth are more likely to develop ADHD.
Numerous studies have demonstrated how exposure to alcohol and cigarette smoke during pregnancy promotes the development of ADHD and other neurological diseases. Exposure to secondhand smoke alone is enough to disrupt a child's developing nervous system. Numerous other contaminants might cause ADHD in the home environment, including pesticides, certain cleaning agents, lead from old paint, and mercury from amalgam fillings.

It is not poor parenting that leads to ADHD, and you cannot cause disorder in your child just by being a lousy parent. The only shaky connection between parenting and ADHD is that many medical professionals firmly believe that ADHD is a hereditary disorder that we can pass on to our children.

You cannot contribute to or cause your child's symptoms, but you can play a significant role in helping him control his hyperactive or inattentive outbursts.

How to assist:
- Take up your child's cause
- Support your child and be conscious of your thoughts
- Consider what others may be thinking.
- Make sure you convey the proper message to your child.
- Keep in mind that you are not to blame.
- The most crucial thing is sorting through all the misconceptions and urban legends concerning ADHD.

HOW TO DETERMINE IF YOUR CHILD HAS ATTENTION DEFICIT HYPERACTIVITY DISORDER:

ADHD SYMPTOMS
Children with ADHD often exhibit behavioral problems such as impulsivity, hyperactivity, distractibility, and lack of focus. Finding the difference between a regular infant or young kid's behavior and ADHD signs can be challenging. How do you tell whether your kid has ADHD for sure?

SYMPTOMS OF ADHD
A youngster typically shows signs of ADHD within the first seven years of life. The primary signs of ADHD include:
- A propensity for aggression.

- The inability to sit still and constant fidgeting.
- Speaking too much, being impatient, and interrupting frequently, are usually done in a loud voice.
- Unable to wait their turn, stand in line, or remain seated.
- Delay in responding to problems.
- Incapable of playing peacefully, they are frequently seen charging, climbing, and dashing.

The list above could seem a little complex at first sight. Who among children doesn't regularly engage in at least one of these activities?

Unfortunately, because there are no clear guidelines, ADHD is rarely immediately or easily diagnosed. You probably have nothing to worry about if your child only occasionally exhibits symptoms of ADHD in particular circumstances. However, additional testing may be necessary if your child consistently exhibits these symptoms, regardless of the circumstance or setting.

HOW TO DIAGNOSE ADHD

Many adults discover ADHD after treatment for another issue, including anxiety or depression. Talking about bad behaviors, problems at work or marital issues frequently indicates that ADHD is to blame. Even if the condition was never diagnosed, it must have been present during childhood to confirm the diagnosis. Childhood issues like lack of focus and hyperactivity can be seen in old report cards or by speaking with family.

One of the fascinating things about ADHD is that a child does not necessarily need to be hyperactive to be diagnosed with it. Inattentional symptoms might also serve as the foundation for an ADHD diagnosis.

Some mental health providers use neuropsychological testing when diagnosing ADHD. These may consist of timed, computer-based assessments that gauge one's capacity for concentration and problem-solving. Although it is not required for diagnosis, neuropsychological testing can provide insight into how ADHD impacts a person's daily life. Additionally, comorbid problems like learning difficulties may be revealed.

All psychiatric disorders, including ADHD, are diagnosed by mental health professionals in the United States using the DSM (Diagnostic and Statistical Manual of Mental Disorders). The most recent version categorizes it into three groups:

- ADHD primarily manifests as inattentive behavior (what used to be called ADD)
- ADHD is primarily manifested as an impulsive behavior
- Mixed presentation of ADHD (both inattentive and hyperactive-impulsive symptoms)

Their particular symptoms will determine the diagnosis for your child.

Despite feeling normal, you keep bumping against an unseen wall. How is it even possible for you to be at ease enough to speak with medical professionals?

Here are two extremely basic keys, and they can assist in making the process easier as you choose the best treatment for your ADHD.

The initial and, in my opinion, most crucial is **moral support.** A huge confidence booster is someone who cares about your well-being and believes in you. It might be a friend, a member of the family, another supporter, or even a participant in a support group. Confidence boosts make communicating with treatment providers much simpler.

The second of these keys **makes talking to your doctor easier.** Doctors are far more receptive to written records than verbal reports from patients. Take this not personally. Trusting you, the patient has nothing to do with it. Doctors are scientists by training.

Additionally, written evidence is far more trustworthy in science than oral testimony. Doctors typically welcome the documentation of a patient's treatment results.

Additionally, it helps speed up the process of getting you the finest possible care. It can also significantly contribute to developing a positive doctor-patient relationship, and it can't hurt that.

Support your inner feelings. Support your doctor's treatment plan from a rational or "scientific" standpoint. There is no better approach to enhance your doctor's interactions with you. Believe me.

Being an adult with ADHD attempting to put together a program for adult ADHD treatment means that you are different from others, and this presents a special set of obstacles. Nobody enjoys being unique. A few people in the general population truly enjoy being different from the norm; only a few are brave enough to step outside that rather rigid and all too comfortable proverbial box.

Nobody values being a cookie-cutter version of anyone else (unless you're a woman carrying a Coach purse). The fact that just ten to twenty-five percent of adults with ADHD seek adult ADHD therapy makes the person seeking it unusual, distinctive, and perhaps not so horrible after all.

The difficulties and annoyances of adult attention deficit hyperactivity disorder are widely known: hyperactivity, impulsivity, lack of focus, lack of attention, etc. Then there are the side consequences, such as deteriorating relationships, falling self-esteem, and failing feelings. The studies do not, however, emphasize a person with ADHD's abilities. No spotlights are shining on the incredibly creative side of an individual with ADHD, no rounds of applause for the passionate pursuit of the individual's many and varied interests, with a never-ending supply of energy.

The research also doesn't highlight the astounding ability to multitask twice as much as a neurotypical individual. Utilizing these assets can help you create an adult ADHD treatment plan that works by focusing on your patient's accomplishments rather than their shortcomings. And that, in and of itself, holds the key to a society that views ADHD not as a disease but rather as a set of traits particular to tremendously interesting and singular people.

Martin Luther famously spoke of a society where diversity was accepted and appreciated. Imagine the potential that people with ADHD could have if their treatment plan were properly carried out: Those with ADHD frequently have incredible levels of energy. Don't lose patience because attending staff meetings feels like your own personal rendition of Chinese water torture. Allow your medical therapy to transform this energy into pure productivity. Hyperactivity can be turned from a nuisance to a benefit by using methods like medication, exercise, and fish oil that reduce restlessness and improve concentration.

Adults with ADHD often have exceptional multitasking skills. Use the ability to switch attention as an advantage by choosing to work on projects or jobs where there is the opportunity to switch multiple times to multiple tasks or where there is the option to complete projects one after the other in quick succession rather than becoming frustrated over the difficulty of focusing on one project long enough to see it through to completion.

Take advantage of the chance to participate in brainstorming sessions actively, give ideas to the workplace (either through suggestion boxes or ideas pushed to your employer), and assist coworkers with their projects. Adults with ADHD are frequently very creative and participate in seeking solutions to challenges and direct their creative energy there.

Become a leader and a motivator. By making meaningful contributions to the lives of the people they love, certain treatments can allow patients to mend connections. Encourage those around you by using your impulsivity to become passionate and enthusiastic about your friends and family's hobbies.

Obey your passions. Adults who have ADHD often have a wide range of interests. Embrace this. Follow these. Don't limit yourself to just one or two interests. Follow two, three, four, five, or six. You will be able to pursue passions with a real interest and satisfaction if adult ADHD treatment can assist in bringing the rest of your life into a healthy balance.

Adults with ADHD don't have to let their impairments define them. With the help of adult ADHD treatment, one can use their condition to their advantage.

ACCURATE ADHD TEST - IS IT POSSIBLE?

Like all mental disorders, ADHD is also difficult to diagnose at times. However, attention deficit hyperactivity disorder can be identified with proper assessment and accurate judgment of the symptoms. Unfortunately, though, this is a time-consuming process, and no ADHD test can at once determine the presence of this serious disorder in a child, adolescent, or adult. It can only be determined after thoroughly studying the patient's social and emotional background.

There is no specific therapist who can diagnose the disorder. Several people, including doctors, mental health professionals, parents, teachers, and peers, have to work together, and only then can the disorder be correctly diagnosed.

A person cannot be diagnosed with the disease immediately after the symptoms surface. The symptoms must last for a minimum of 6 months before ADHD can even be considered a problem.

HOW THE ADHD TESTS WORK:
For the disorder's successful diagnosis, several ADHD tests must be carried out simultaneously.

Since hyperactivity, impulsivity, and inattentiveness are the hallmarks of ADHD, therapists must diagnose their patients with the condition appropriately. This is because most children naturally exhibit all three of the characteristics above. As a result, only after careful examination of the symptoms' frequency, intensity, and severity can an accurate diagnosis of attention deficit hyperactivity disorder be made.

If a child has to be evaluated for ADHD, the pediatrician should be consulted first. Some pediatricians can perform the tests themselves, but others will refer the young patient to a licensed psychiatrist. The two doctors then compare notes and interview the child's family members, including parents, teachers, and friends, to learn more about the severity of the symptoms, when they first appeared, etc.

The child's past is carefully investigated. When a youngster exhibits signs of ADHD due to either emotional (family death, stress) or physical (learning disabilities, hearing problems) causes, ADHD is typically ruled out.

Therefore, it is evident that locating and combining reliable ADHD tests can significantly aid in diagnosing and managing the condition. The treatment of ADHD is now much more accessible than it was a few years ago, thanks to some highly promising alternative drugs that are readily available. Get a proper diagnosis, pick a sensible course of treatment, and proceed with your battle against the disorder.

TREATMENTS FOR ADHD IN CHILDREN

Medication that contains stimulants, such as methylphenidate, is the basis of treatment for ADHD (Ritalin). Although there are few long-term trials, several short-term ones have demonstrated the safety and efficacy of these medicines. While stimulant addiction in teenagers has been documented in those without ADHD, it is extremely uncommon in those with the disorder. Stimulants don't give someone with ADHD a "high" feeling; they only help them feel normal.

Most children with ADHD require a structured educational setting and a behavioral modification program that can help them learn how to control their disruptive or aggressive behaviors. Hence, a collaborative effort between parents, therapists, and teachers is crucial. Finally, a combination of medication and counseling may be helpful for individuals with ADHD.

Those with ADHD may require assistance with life organization. Thus, a few straightforward treatments to attempt for childhood ADHD include:

Establish a schedule. Ensure that your child follows the same schedule every day. Time for play and homework should be included in the schedule, and this timetable should be displayed prominently inside the house.

Assist your child in organizing common items. Create an organized space with your youngster. Clothing, rucksacks, and school supplies fall under this category.

A digital therapy tool called EndeavorRx, which has been found to help treat ADHD in children aged 8 to 12, has also received FDA approval. The system tests the child's movement skills and stimulates brain regions to help with better brain function, much like a video game.

Keep in mind that kids with ADHD want guidelines they can readily follow that are constant. Rewarding your youngster for following the rules is important.

It might be challenging to distinguish between ADHD symptoms and typical child misbehavior. The process of diagnosing takes time and typically involves observation over several days or weeks to evaluate the surroundings and circumstances surrounding any problematic behavior.

Not all children with ADHD are 'crazy' or hyperactive; the illness can also exist in more reserved kids. Keep a notebook if you begin to feel uneasy. This will be helpful for any future expert consultations and give you a decent indication of whether or not you should be concerned.

The first person you should contact if you suspect your child may have ADHD is their teacher. Teachers are typically the first to detect if anything is wrong because all three of the major indications have an impact on learning.

ADHD THERAPIES FOR ADULTS

One or more of the following therapies may be used to treat adult ADHD:

Individuals may benefit from cognitive and behavioral therapy to alter unhelpful thought patterns and raise self-esteem.

To lessen tension and anxiety, use relaxation techniques.

Using behavioral coaching, teach students how to plan their daily activities at home and work.

Job coaching or mentoring to promote better working relationships and enhance performance while on the job

WHAT IS THE SUGGESTED TREATMENT FOR ADHD IN TEENS?

When it comes to managing teen ADHD, there are a variety of viewpoints. According to some experts, teenagers may benefit from behavior therapy alone.

However, the National Institute of Mental Health reports that roughly 80% of people who need medication for ADHD as children continue to do so as teenagers.

The most effective treatment for ADHD in teenagers is typically a combination of medication and behavior therapy. Behavior therapy is advised to treat the behavioral issues associated with ADHD.

Teens with ADHD are frequently treated with stimulant medicines. Teens who use these medicines may become more awake and do better in the classroom. Lisdexamfetamine (Vyvanse), dexmethylphenidate (Focalin, Focalin X.R.), dextroamphetamine (Adderall, Adderall X.R.), methylphenidate (Quillivant XR, Concerta, Ritalin), and mixed salts of a single-entity amphetamine product,(Mydayis), are a few examples of stimulant drugs.

Teens with ADHD can also be treated with non-stimulant drugs, including atomoxetine (Strattera), clonidine (Kapvay), guanfacine

(Intuniv), and viloxazine (Qelbree). The side effects of non-stimulant ADHD treatments are distinct from those of stimulant drugs. For instance, unlike stimulant medicines, they don't frequently cause anxiety, agitation, or insomnia. They may be a better alternative for teenagers with ADHD who struggle with alcohol or drug abuse because they don't establish habits and are less likely to be abused than stimulant medications.

Overmedication doesn't work and can result in drug abuse, suicidal thoughts, and mood swings.

Elimination diets, supplement use, parent training, memory training, and neurofeedback are a few alternative therapies. Sometimes these procedures are combined with taking prescribed drugs.

The advantages of omega-3 fatty acids have also been demonstrated. The FDA recently approved a tiny device to aid in stimulating the area of the brain thought to be responsible for ADHD. Patients aged 7 to 12 who are not taking ADHD medication may be prescribed this device, known as the Monarch External Trigeminal Nerve Stimulation (eTNS) System.

ADULT ADHD MEDICATION FOR DEPRESSION

Adults frequently use stimulant medications with ADHD (attention deficit hyperactivity disorder) to treat their symptoms. However, your doctor could advise you to try an antidepressant if you don't feel better after taking those medications or if you don't like how they make you feel.

Not everyone has the same effects from stimulants like methylphenidate (Ritalin) or dextroamphetamine and amphetamine (Adderall). It's possible that your symptoms won't go away, or you'll experience negative effects like nausea, trouble sleeping, or jitteriness.

THE EFFECTS OF ANTIDEPRESSANTS ON ADHD SYMPTOMS

Antidepressant medications increase the amounts of brain neurotransmitters like dopamine and norepinephrine, just like stimulants do. These medications, according to doctors, can help people living with ADHD increase their attention span, and they also aid in controlling impulsive, hyperactive, or violent behavior.

Some adults with ADHD also experience anxiety and depression. If that applies to you, antidepressant medications may be an option, as they can treat both these issues and ADHD.

ADULT ADHD ANTIDEPRESSANTS: TYPES OF MEDICINES

Although doctors frequently use antidepressants to treat ADHD, the FDA has not given its approval for that use. Your doctor might advise one of the following four:

Inhibitors of monoamine oxidase, such as bupropion (Wellbutrin) (MAOIs)

Venlafaxine and other tricyclic antidepressants such as desipramine (Norpramin) and imipramine (Tofranil) (Effexor)

Based on your unique symptoms and other medical issues, you should choose the best antidepressant for you.

Remember that it can take up to four weeks for antidepressants to start functioning. Even if you first don't see any change in symptoms, it's crucial to adhere to your doctor's advice for how frequently to take them.

Antidepressants typically don't work as well at enhancing focus or attention span as stimulants and other medications designed particularly to treat ADHD. But each person's performance varies. Antidepressants may be quite beneficial for some people with ADHD.

Some people shouldn't use antidepressants. For instance, if you have a history of manic behavior brought on by bipolar disorder, they might not be accurate. Additionally, taking Wellbutrin is not advised if you have ever had a seizure or have a history of epilepsy.

ANTIDEPRESSANT SIDE EFFECTS

The sort of antidepressant medication you're taking may impact the adverse effects.

Tricyclic antidepressants, for instance, have been linked to some heart problems, as adverse effects include a quicker heart rate and increased blood pressure. Wellbutrin may result in rashes, headaches, and anxiety, and MAOIs might lead to weight gain and sleep issues. Constipation and upset stomach are additional side effects that antidepressants may cause. You can experience sweating, dizziness, sleepiness, and blurred vision. Other potential issues include:

- mouth ache
- Loss of weight
- reduced blood pressure

- Tremors

Inform your doctor of any past health issues, especially those that may have affected your ability to take certain antidepressants, such as heart issues, seizures, or high blood pressure.

Additionally, if you skip a dose or don't take an antidepressant exactly as directed, you may experience withdrawal symptoms or other negative effects. When using these medications, be sure to follow your doctor's directions.

LONG-TERM SIDE EFFECTS OF ADULT ADHD DRUGS

Drugs for ADHD have been studied in adults far less extensively than in children, although the results are encouraging. According to studies, adults who take stimulants experience fewer symptoms of ADHD, and some people report being able to concentrate better after around 30 minutes.

It's time to get your ADHD under control now that you've seen your doctor and made that decision. But you might be curious whether the medication you require is long-term safe.

If you're an adult, the majority of your long-term concerns about ADHD medications relate to how they may impact other medical disorders you may have.

Following an examination by your doctor, you can develop a strategy that will keep you healthy and improve your concentration.

Long-term usage of ADHD medication is connected with the following risks and side effects:

- Heart condition
- elevated blood pressure
- Seizure
- abnormal heartbeat
- Abuse and dependency
- Skin imperfections
- Heart disease or hypertension
- Stimulants are the most popular types of ADHD medications. It may seem ironic that stimulants are used to treat hyperactive or restless people, and these medications may improve attention span and reduce distractibility by adjusting attention-related brain circuits. Your doctor may give an antidepressant to stabilize mood or a selective norepinephrine reuptake inhibitor, such as atomoxetine, which can help regulate impulsive behaviors if stimulants are insufficiently effective.

Most medications for ADHD are stimulants, and they have the power to increase heart rate and blood pressure. These medications may be hazardous if you already have a cardiac condition. Examples comprise:
- Amphetamine (Evekeo)
- Dextroamphetamine (Adderall, Adderall X.R., Dexedrine, ProCentra, Zenzedi)
- Dexmethylphenidate (Focalin, Focalin X.R.)
- Lisdexamfetamine (Vyvanse)
- Methylphenidate (Concerta, Daytrana, Metadate, Methylin, Ritalin, Quillivant)

1. A seizure or a fast or slow heartbeat

Atomoxetine (Strattera), a different ADHD medicine that isn't a stimulant, has been connected to seizures and irregular heartbeats. The FDA advises against using it if you have a history of those issues.

2. Abuse or Dependence

Some people abuse stimulant medications for ADHD. They might shatter the pills and snort them to get high, resulting in a potentially fatal overdose.

It's improbable that you'll follow that path if you don't have a history of substance misuse. But if you do, you run the risk of abusing your ADHD medications.

Tell your doctor about any substance misuse you've done in the past or now. They can assist you in determining whether or not you should take ADHD medications.

3. Psychiatric Conditions

Drugs for ADHD may occasionally cause mental health problems; however, this is uncommon. For instance, some persons have complained about aggressive and hostile conduct issues. Others claim that they started to exhibit bipolar illness symptoms.

The FDA has additionally cautioned that there is a tiny possibility that stimulant ADHD medications could cause mood swings or psychotic symptoms, such as hearing things and paranoia.

4. A discolored complexion

Chemical leukoderma, a skin ailment, has been linked to the methylphenidate transdermal system (Daytrana) skin patch. The disorder results in a permanent loss of skin pigmentation at the patched area.

HOW TO CONSIDER RISKS

Consult your physician. You can determine if taking ADHD medications is safe for you together.

To determine whether you have any illnesses that might not interact well with ADHD medications, your doctor may order a few tests. See if you have an irregular pulse, high blood pressure, or other forms of heart disease, for instance.

Additional conditions may increase your risks from medication for ADHD. If you have one of these, let your doctor know:
- Sensitivity or allergy to stimulants
- Glaucoma
- a kidney or liver condition
- previous mental illness
- Tourette's syndrome or motor tics
- unbalanced thyroid

If you take any additional medications or dietary supplements, let them know. With ADHD medications, some people may react poorly.

Once you take your ADHD medication, schedule routine checkups with your doctor to ensure you aren't experiencing any negative side effects.

Remember that ADHD drugs are generally safe, and the risksare low. For lots of people, the benefits of treatment outweigh the risks.

LIFE FOLLOWING AN ADHD DIAGNOSIS

When you are given an ADHD diagnosis, it can be very daunting.

Hopefully, you have mostly pleasant thoughts about it. In some ways, years or decades of disappointment and errors now make a lot of sense. There is also solace in learning that many problematic behaviors and bad habits that have interfered with your progress in school, work, and personal life are the product of a different neurological organization of brain tissue. It's only biological.

However, adjusting to the ADHD diagnosis and treatment regimen can sometimes be difficult. Some people could feel lost and unsure of what to do in a strange landscape, and others could feel overloaded with information. The most crucial thing is to gradually acclimate to your new normal concept and seek out what makes you feel comfortable. To get you there, consider the following recommendations from the beginning.

BREATHE, THEN ENGAGE IN CONVERSATION

Please take a few days to consider your diagnosis when you receive it. This diagnosis will frequently follow one, or even a few, earlier misdiagnoses. This is because secondary symptoms of ADHD, such as anxiety or sadness, may first be mistaken for the primary problem. After giving them some thought, write down all your questions for your doctor, then go back to develop a treatment strategy. A nutritious diet, regular exercise, sound sleep habits, meditation, coaching, and/or medication are all beneficial for most ADHD sufferers.

Ask for an explanation if your doctor has strong feelings about a specific detail, and be forthright if you disagree. See a second opinion or a physician with more experience treating adult ADHD if interested. There is no harm in asking, and building a reliable and cozy support system is what matters most.

Regarding second opinions, this might be a choice made more frequently by women than by males due to the sad, pervasive myth that women do not have ADHD. This misconception has been disproven, but every year, women with ADHD are misdiagnosed despite this.

One final thing to remember about the medical side of diagnosis: don't anticipate immediate outcomes. Be flexible when changing your treatment plan and observe what functions well and doesn't, but be aware that it sometimes takes an ADHDer longer than six months to feel like things are improving. Persevere! In the long run, it will be profitable.

EQUIP YOURSELF WITH KNOWLEDGE

Federal laws protect people with ADHD; one of the most significant prohibits unfair job termination. That is only one of the facts that every person with ADHD should be aware of.

For those with ADHD, much information is available—so much so that it can be overwhelming. Recall your preferred learning method, take a step back, and let that lead you. For those who learn best visually, there are books like this, films and slideshows, blogs for those who learn best via anecdotes, and live support groups and counselors (and, of course, ADHD coaches) for those who prefer one-on-one attention or a sounding board.

Whichever resource you choose, you'll find a wide range of recommendations on treatment strategies, reducing negative behavioral difficulties, changing poor habits, minimizing secondary

ADHD symptoms in your life, and generally moving forward to a healthier place.

DIAGNOSIS DISCLOSURE
Who to tell is one of the touchiest issues in the weeks following an ADHD diagnosis. Your response may determine how you inform your family, friends, and coworkers; someone relieved by their diagnosis may want to tell everyone, while someone dissatisfied with their diagnosis may wish to keep it a secret. In either case, it is a sensitive issue that requires extra care.

In general, it's a good idea to tell your family and close friends that you have ADHD. Your treatment plan will call for adjustments to your routines and habits, and because their lives will also be touched, they should have the chance to learn more. They'll probably also want to encourage you and be there for you. Family members can assist in monitoring side effects or negative reactions for ADHD patients prescribed medication as needed.

Most significantly, you will experience an emotional and difficult shift from being a captive of the uncontrollable consequences of ADHD to a self-controlled and healthy person. Count on the affection and support of the people you care about. To help them overcome any outmoded misconceptions, they may still harbor in their thoughts, share the knowledge you have gained about ADHD. Please include them in the process and give them the resources to support you.

It can be more difficult to bring up ADHD with coworkers and superiors. It's one thing if Great Aunt Margaret makes a sarcastic quip at Thanksgiving every year and never bothered to study up on ADHD, and it's quite different if such a reaction occurs at work when it may impact your livelihood. There is no requirement under law to disclose your ailment to your employer. It may be advisable to start your treatment plan discreetly and wait for improvements in your work performance to happen spontaneously because, in many circumstances, actions speak louder than words.

Be calm and positive when you decide to inform someone. They will learn how to think and communicate about ADHD from how you talk about it. Acting embarrassed or sorry sends the message that ADHD is something to be ashamed of. Instead, walk them through your response to influence theirs. For instance, "At first, I was scared that I would be labeled, but the more I thought about it and read about it, the more sense it made, and now I'm pleased that I can work through the attention issues that have affected me from childhood." Remain upbeat and discuss the causes and effects of your diagnosis. Be clear about what you require or anticipate from them so that they are prepared to assist you.

AN EXCITING NEW FUTURE

It is not easy to adjust to life with well-managed ADHD. It includes changing a lot of old habits and adopting some new ones. It also involves having the people in your life see you in a new manner and allowing you to see yourself from a new perspective. During these first few months of life after your diagnosis, remember to give yourself time, be disciplined with your treatment plan, and push the boundaries of your comfort zone. And one more thing - soon, you will have more tools to use to live your life on your terms.

FAQ ABOUT ADHD MEDICATION

The most frequent inquiries people have about ADHD drugs follow a disorder diagnosis. Even though we have been treating ADHD with the same psychostimulants for over 60 years and have repeatedly examined their efficacy, short- and long-term side effects, and contraindications, uncertainty still exists.

Here is a summary of the three most frequently asked questions about ADHD medication and the most common misconceptions they address. This information is provided to assist people in making informed decisions about their treatment options.

WHAT DRUGS ARE PRESCRIBED TO TREAT ADHD?

There are two main types of ADHD medications: stimulants and non-stimulants. Ritalin, Adderall, Concerta, Dexedrine, Focalin, Metadate, and Vyvanse are examples of brands for stimulants. The dopamine in the brains of those with ADHD is "stimulated" by these drugs, rebalancing the dopamine imbalance that normally exists and contributes to the symptoms of ADHD. The brand names of common non-stimulants for treating ADHD include Strattera, Wellbutrin, Effexor, Clonidine, and Intuniv. These are hypothesized to indirectly lessen the symptoms of ADHD by acting on other neurotransmitters in the body or the brain.

There isn't a "miracle cure" or "cure-all" for ADHD. This suggests that people still function best when they develop techniques to manage other areas that still challenge them, even though drugs have been shown to lessen 80% of the symptoms. It's crucial to remember that most ADHD drugs do not stay active in your body continuously throughout the day, and most drugs normally last 4 to 8 hours. The rest of the day and on the weekends, you continue to have ADHD. The best results are achieved when medications are combined with training in skills and management techniques to handle your issues better. Along with medicine, strategies including behavior modification, biofeedback, coaching, psychotherapy, and support groups are just a few options.

WHY ARE "STIMULANTS" UTILIZED WHEN HYPERACTIVITY IS THE ISSUE?

The physical hyperactivity in behavior that some people with ADHD exhibit is essentially a sign of mental inactivity. The body's physical movement helps to enhance the dopamine available to the brain when people are hyperactive, active, and restless. ADHD is thought to be primarily caused by a lack of dopamine reaching the brain's frontal lobe.

The capacity to pay attention, focus on less exciting things, halt before acting, etc., is practically difficult when this front part of the brain, or "executive function," is not completely accessible. It's similar to assuming that someone with vision problems will "concentrate" to see better—that won't happen! When we walk, our brain is stimulated to release dopamine. Because the individual no longer has to move around, the symptoms are lessened when more dopamine is accessible to excite these important areas of the brain.

ARE DRUGS PRESCRIBED FOR ADHD SAFE? CAN THEY LEAD TO ADDICTION?

As shocking as it may sound, ADHD has been treated with stimulant medication for over 60 years. Since the 1950s, Ritalin has been used to treat symptoms similar to ADHD. They have been used for a long time and have been widely researched, allowing us to understand their long-term impacts through generations. They are as "safe" as any drug can be. Numerous studies have found that people taking prescription medicines are less likely to abuse other drugs since they don't need to start looking for alternative ways to self-medicate their symptoms.

HOW DO PHYSICIANS IDENTIFY ADHD?

Your child's physician will use the Diagnostic and Statistical Manual (DSM-5) of the American Psychiatric Association (APA) to diagnose

ADHD. The guidebook guarantees that children receive appropriate therapy for their ailment and outlines rules for diagnosis criteria.

Your child must exhibit a pattern of inattention and/or hyperactivity-impulsivity to be diagnosed with ADHD. These symptoms must adversely impact the development of your child.

Your youngster must exhibit six or more signs of the inattentive kind (for kids up to 16) or five or more signs (for older kids) (for those 17 and older). These need to be present for a minimum of six months. They consist of the following:

- Lacks attention to detail or makes careless errors
- Has trouble sustaining attention during tasks and appears not to listen to others when they speak
- does not carry out the instructions
- Organizational actions are problematic
- avoids or dislikes tasks that require sustained mental effort
- tends to misplace important items
- Is easily distracted Forgetful while performing daily tasks

Your child must exhibit six or more signs of hyperactivity and impulsivity for children up to 16 or five or more for those 17 and older for at least six months. These signs include:

- tends to tap their feet or hands or fidget with them
- frequently gets up from their seat (in situations where it is inappropriate)
- runs or climbs in inappropriate locations and cannot play or participate in activities without making noise
- seems to be constantly moving.
- Talks a lot and answers quickly before the question is ended
- has trouble waiting for their turn.
- Tends to cut other people off

To receive a diagnosis, your child must also:

- Before the age of twelve, many of these symptoms
- signs displayed in many contexts (school, extracurricular activities, home, etc.)
- Symptoms affecting their ability to perform well
- There is no illness that more accurately describes their symptoms.

HOW TO QUICKLY RECOGNIZE THE ADHD SYMPTOMS

To a large extent, ADHD can be cured with early detection and subsequent therapy. The most typical signs and symptoms of ADHD are listed below. Unfortunately, many parents are uninformed about the specific signs and symptoms of ADHD, so kids don't get the right care. Learn more about the disease's truths and myths by reading on. It is crucial to raise awareness about ADHD because it is becoming a more common disease in youngsters.

- Hyperactivity: If you observe that your child has trouble sitting still, is agitated, or talks or moves around continually, even when engaged in a task, they may have attention deficit hyperactivity disorder.
- Lack of attention: This is another significant sign of ADHD. Children find it difficult to focus, are frequently distracted in their imaginations (dreaming of improbable things), and seldom obey directions. Attention deficit hyperactivity disorder (ADHD) may affect kids who find it difficult to focus, get bored easily, or nearly always miss school.
- Impulsivity: ADHD is more likely to afflict kids exhibiting this symptom. They also say inappropriate and subpar things at the wrong times. Because the child lacks emotional control, this happens. An impulsive child typically struggles to wait their time during sports or performances and is unconcerned with the repercussions of bad behavior.

The most typical signs of ADHD are those. The symptoms might range from being highly obvious in some circumstances to much less so in others. It is possible to separate or mix symptoms. The two most obvious of the three symptoms listed are hyperactivity and impulsivity. It can be challenging to identify the sign of inattention, though. This youngster generally has low moods, gets along well with peers, and doesn't exhibit many behavioral issues.

The following points should be noted as you check for signs of attention deficit hyperactivity:

1. Before ADHD can be diagnosed, the child must experience symptoms for at least six months.
2. Not every child who exhibits impulsivity, hyperactivity, or both may have ADHD. But it must never be disregarded. A check can quickly identify the illness and aid in the healing process.
3. Impulsive children can be mistaken for individuals experiencing emotional issues, which isn't usually the case. As was already noted, any uncertainty should be cleared up as soon as possible because the prompt diagnosis can greatly increase the likelihood of a child's full recovery.

A youngster with ADHD must receive safe and healthful treatment. Harmful chemical medications can have a significant impact on kids' physical activity. Take your child to a therapist who gently addresses the issue as soon as the symptoms have been discovered. Homeopathy is one alternative medication that is becoming more and more well-liked. Consider the options available, and assist your child in fully recovering and maintaining their health.

MYTH ABOUT ADHD

The origins of ADHD are still mostly unknown, and researchers are continuallylooking into the condition to learn more about it. There are numerous widespread misconceptions about ADHD.

First, diet or sugar consumption in children does not cause ADHD. Many false claims that sugar makes kids hyper have been made. There is no proven link between sugar and ADHD, according to scientific studies. According to studies, just 5% of children with ADHD benefited from a diet change. According to research, sugar has no impact on children's behavior or development.

ADHD is not brought on by watching TV, and no research has demonstrated a connection between childhood and ADHD.

Families and parenting do not cause ADHD. The presence of ADHD is a medical illness, and parenting abilities or deficiencies cannot alter this fact.

However, due to the negative views toward an ADHD child that may be expressed by parents or expressed by strangers witnessing an ADHD child act out, parents of ADHD children are frequently perceived as being bad parents. Children with ADHD are frequently disobedient, which makes those outside the family assume that the child is not being properly parented.

Researchers have discovered that executive function-controlling brain regions are affected by ADHD, a medical disorder. Memory, planning, organization, behavior, and thinking are all examples of executive functions, but they are not the only ones. None of the abovementioned fallacies apply to the specific genes and chemicals linked to ADHD.

The misconceptions around ADHD are more widely spread than the actual statistics. Unfortunately, a lot of the material that is available about ADHD is simply false and deceptive. You need proper information as a parent of a child with ADHD so that you can support your efforts to help your child succeed in life.

Let's examine some of the most prevalent and widely conjectured falsehoods concerning ADHD.

- ADHD is a result of poor parenting.
- We're all a little bit ADHD (some of the time).
- Food influences ADHD.
- Drugs can treat ADHD.
- Drug companies design drugs to treat ADHD.

- Dishonest mental health professionals make up ADHD for financial gain.
- Children require more control.
- When I was younger, ADHD didn't exist.

While some of these have compelling arguments, they share the same trait. They are all untrue and misguided. Every "myth" has some truth to it, I think, but when it comes to ADHD, they are all seriously deceptive.

The following are some myths regarding ADHD and the information that dispels them:

MYTH: Only boys are impacted by ADHD.

FACT: There is no evidence to conclude that either sex is more likely to be impacted by ADHD than the other, and boys and girls are equally likely to be afflicted.

MYTH: ADHD eventually fades from the lives of kids.

FACT: About 70% of kids with ADHD will still suffer symptoms throughout adolescence, and 60% will continue to have symptoms into adulthood.

Myth: ADHD is transient

A lifelong disorder with a hereditary basis, Attention Deficit Hyperactivity Disorder tends to run in families, according to reputable medical research. So there can be no adult-onset ADHD. Despite having ADHD as children, the women diagnosed as adults managed to deal with their ADHD-like symptoms, sometimes effectively and sometimes not.

ADHD typically manifests at a breaking point, such as when someone changes jobs, gets divorced, or even goes through menopause. Overwhelming the coping methods that previously served them well allows for a delayed ADHD diagnosis.

Bottom line: Women who successfully manage their ADHD can establish new habits, enhance their life strategies, and take the right medications, but they will still exhibit ADHD-like behaviors. ADHD persists forever. But ADHD is a lifestyle, not a life sentence.

Myth: ADHD therapy is a continuous, painless procedure.

ADHD is unpredictable by its very nature; focus shifts frequently. Adults with ADHD are easily bored and demand frequent changes in context or subject; the same is true of ADD treatment. Finding the ideal drug mix, behavioral adjustments, and structure may take months or even years.

The tenacity of a bulldog describes women with ADHD. Other than on themselves, they hardly ever give up. It's simple for them to become disheartened by the slow pace of ADHD therapy after a lifetime of futile tries and false starts.

Conclusion: Treatment effectiveness will fluctuate like a roller coaster. There will be some home runs and foul balls when trying different therapies, diets, exercises, and supplements. Amazing results are possible, but they demand time and a little bit of patience.

Myth: You can "cure" ADHD on your own.

Many ADHD women choose to live in seclusion. They don't want people to see how dirty their homes are or learn that they never arrive at work on time. Because of their loneliness, they constantly tell themselves they aren't good enough or that other people don't want to be their friends or companions.

Women sometimes escape back to the shelter alone when they realize that a round of medicine or greater willpower won't make their ADHD go away. But ADHD-afflicted women require the assistance of other females who genuinely comprehend the psychological effects of ADHD. They need to be aware that they are not the only ones who wash their clothes again (again!) after forgetting to put them in the dryer. Those who talk too much while paying too little attention.

MYTH: If you weren't diagnosed with ADHD as a child, you can't have it as an adult.

FACT: Some kids grow up with incomplete or incorrect diagnoses, and others can manage their symptoms as children, delaying the full onset or recognition of their problems until maturity. The diagnosis of ADHD is, therefore, common and accurate.

MYTH: Adults with ADHD cannot be properly diagnosed.

FACT: There isn't a single test for diagnosing adult ADHD. Both the DSM and the American Medical Association provide detailed descriptions of the symptoms of ADHD in both adults and children, and medical professionals are required to follow certain diagnostic criteria when making such diagnoses.

MYTH: Those who have ADHD are illiterate and lazy.

FACT: Many persons with ADHD are more intelligent than the typical person. However, the symptoms brought on by brain imbalances give the affected person a look of stupidity or laziness. It's believed that many legendary figures suffered from ADHD. Successfully managing their disorders has allowed some to become CEOs and owners of organizations still in business.

MYTH: Everyone eventually develops symptoms of ADHD, but smart individuals can get over them.
FACT: ADHD and intelligence are unrelated. Many people who have ADHD are incredibly bright. Anyone can encounter ADHD symptoms. Without ADHD, it's typically brought on by excessive stimulation, attitude, mood, or exhaustion. People with ADHD experience chronic impairment as a result of their symptoms.
MYTH: Someone with ADHD can't experience depression, anxiety, or psychiatric issues.
FACT: An individual with ADHD has a sixfold increased risk of developing another psychiatric or learning issue.
MYTH: Taking medicine for ADHD leads to drug misuse.
FACT: It has been established that the prescription medicine used to treat ADHD is safe and effective. Untreated ADHD patients are more likely to take drugs because of their addictive tendencies, and getting treated lowers the risk.
Myth: ADHD is a brand-new condition impacting youngsters today. We have been aware of ADHD since the early 1900s, several decades ago. Before that, the illness could not be diagnosed using any diagnostic criteria.
Nevertheless, it is safe to presume that the condition impacted many great people in history, even before 1900, based on the current diagnostic criteria and the writings and information on numerous prominent and influential past people. For instance, Albert Einstein, Christopher Columbus, and Abraham Lincoln are all well-known examples of people who may have had ADHD.
MYTH: Special classes must be set up for kids with ADHD.
FALSE! Beware of anyone who offers this ADHD advice. The effects of ADHD are not felt in an intellectual capacity. However, many children with ADHD also have learning difficulties, necessitating strategies like positive reinforcement, an organized study schedule, and engaging learning materials.
Myth: Children with ADHD merely make up reasons for their actions rather than accepting accountability.
Truth: Therapists, doctors, and educators view ADHD as a problem rather than a justification for poor performance. The medication used to treat ADHD helps the child's specific chemical imbalance, and these drugs give kids with ADHD a chance at leading regular lives devoid of the issues brought on by their condition.
Myth: Poor parenting is the cause of ADHD.

Truth: It's a frequent misconception that children with ADHD are simply unruly brats whose parents are unable or unwilling to discipline them. More discipline or stricter discipline alone does not improve the condition, according to tests; in fact, the issue worsens.

Parenting abilities, or a lack of parenting abilities, are not to blame for children's ADHD because it is a biological illness that affects the frontal lobes of the brain (as is evident in CAT and MRI scans). Unfortunately, many parents are left with the impression that they are to blame for their child's (or children's) diagnosis of this condition.

Myth: Giving Children Ritalin is dangerous.

The fact is that Ritalin is a highly effective treatment for ADHD in both children and adults, as shown by several research studies. Ritalin has been used successfully to treat ADHD for over 50 years with no significant long-term negative effects. While it would be inaccurate to claim no negative effects, taking too much Ritalin has never resulted in a fatality. Ritalin does not influence growth, and children who eventually stop taking it do not have any negative side effects that last a lifetime.

Myth: There is no such thing as ADHD.

Truth: Attention Deficit Hyperactivity Disorder, also known as ADHD, is a neurobiological disorder that the courts have accepted, the U.S. Department of Education, the U.S. Congress, the NIH (National Institutes of Health), and all major medical specialties, including physicians, psychiatric doctors, and educational associations.

Thanks greatly to advances in science and technology, we now understand that this disease is a real condition. According to CAT and MRI tests, the brains of a youngster with the illness and a child without it differ noticeably.

Myth: Giving a youngster Ritalin is like giving them cocaine.

Truth: Although Ritalin, also known as methylphenidate, is a stimulant, it differs chemically from cocaine, an illegal narcotic. Ritalin is not addictive or physically dependent when used as a prescribed medicine, and it prevents the patient from going into psychosis.

Myth: Over time, ADHD may be overcome.

Truth: ADHD affects adults and children, with adult cases increasing. Children diagnosed with ADHD between 15 and 50 percent of the time might always have the condition.

People with ADHD can live a relatively normal, contented life with proper diagnosis and treatment. The fallacies surrounding this condition are standard; people will always disagree with an emotional disorder.

Speak with your child's doctor and inquire about the disease to further inform yourself. Your understanding of the illness will improve, and any misconceptions you may encounter will be dispelled with the assistance of a specialist.

However, more experts and parents today chose to skip medicine in favor of alternative treatment choices. Treatment often consists of medication and therapy. Many alternative therapies are proving to be quite effective, and some even result in changes that seem to last even after they are stopped. But when using treatments that appear to be natural, it's advisable to err on the side of caution. Something's safety cannot be assured just because it is natural. Discuss this with your child's mental health practitioner before starting a treatment program, especially if they are already taking ADHD medication.

MYTHS ABOUT NATURAL ADHD SUPPLEMENTS

Have you ever considered using natural treatments for ADHD? Natural ADHD pills are becoming increasingly popular, but many individuals are still dubious about the phenomenon since they trust all the false information.

Here are five widespread misconceptions about natural ADHD supplements debunked.

1. Prescription stimulants are more successful than natural treatments for ADHD in youngsters. While some people continue to use stimulants, many parents are understandably concerned about possible negative effects. Many believe that natural treatments are gentler and, therefore, less effective. Yet, studies demonstrate that, in most circumstances, they can produce similarly encouraging outcomes without the negative side effects associated with using stimulants!
2. Natural ADHD supplements are highly pricey. You will be astonished at how much less expensive a homeopathic treatment is than a prescription stimulant if you find one that is both effective and economical.

    Natural ADHD pills will help you address your child's condition while saving you a ton of money and enhancing your general health.
3. Diet has no bearing on ADHD. Although there are some doubters, statistics support the effectiveness of dietary

changes as a natural treatment for ADHD in children. The signs of ADHD might be lessened by eating a nutritious diet. Many kids consume an excessive amount of processed and junk food. The symptoms of ADHD can be made worse by food allergies like sugar and MSG. Nutritional deficiencies, such as those in the B-complex vitamins and minerals, can potentially contribute to ADHD symptoms.

4. Only prescription stimulants can treat ADHD; natural supplements cannot. Numerous parents erroneously think stimulants are a panacea for ADHD; in reality, they are merely a band-aid that masks the symptoms.

   Your child's problems will reappear if he stops taking his prescription medication. However, because they approach the issue holistically and deal with the potential root causes of your child's ADHD, natural treatments for ADHD, like homeopathy, get the closest to a cure.

5. Businesses that market all-natural treatments for ADHD are merely after your money. ADHD in youngsters can be treated naturally, and this is nothing new. Nowadays, ADHD is significantly more prevalent due to the bad food and lifestyle that many kids pursue.

   Natural medicine businesses are merely offering an alternative to harsh conventional treatment. If you only read some studies and patient testimonials, it won't take long to discover that natural therapies like homeopathy work for many individuals.

There you have it, then. These are a few of the widespread misconceptions regarding natural supplements for ADHD. Natural treatments can assist you if you want to assist your youngster in permanently recovering from ADHD.

They are not quack remedies, as you may believe. Once you do a little checking, you'll see that they do work for a lot of people. Never give in to pressure from anyone, not even your doctor, to give your child prescription medication. Homeopathy is a natural remedy that is far safer and more economical than prescription drugs.

MYTHS ABOUT DRUGS FOR ADHD

All of us have heard about the debate surrounding Ritalin and other ADHD drugs. The negative effects that medications like Ritalin are known to cause in many kids are included in the facts regarding ADHD.

Although the FDA has approved these medications, they also include extremely severe warnings, known as the "black box warning," on the labels. This shows that the medicine in question is hazardous and must always be taken under adult supervision. Some kids will sell the ADHD meds they are taking to other kids they know. This is because college students use ADHD drugs to help them lose weight and stay alert as they study for examinations. Others are ashamed and don't want their friends to know they have to take medication for ADHD.

Now, drugs with extended-release guarantee your child will benefit from the medication all day long and won't need to take a dose while at school.

Since some high school and college students claim they use prescription stimulants like Adderall and Ritalin to help them study more effectively or party longer, these medicines have received much media attention lately. Inappropriate use of prescription stimulants, which are typically recommended to treat attention deficit hyperactivity disorder (ADHD), can have detrimental effects on one's health.

Here are five misconceptions regarding prescribed stimulants.

Myth 1: Substances like Ritalin and Adderall can increase your intelligence.

It's a fact that while these medicines may help you focus, they won't help you study more or get better marks.

Being "smart" is about developing your capacity to grasp novel concepts, abilities, and ideas. The brain may be exercised to grow stronger, much like a muscle. Through experience and repetition, learning forges stronger brain connections that improve cognition—or "smartness"—throughout a lifetime. Abusing prescription stimulants is an example of a shortcut that does not "exercise" the brain.

According to research, college and high school kids who abuse prescription stimulants have poorer GPAs than those who don't.

Myth #2: Stimulants on prescription are mere "brain vitamins."

Contrary to vitamins, these medications comprise components that might alter brain chemistry and cause severe negative effects.

Additionally, they need a prescription from a doctor, unlike vitamins. You are misusing the medicine and risk becoming addicted if you take it more frequently than recommended, in higher doses, or any other method besides orally.

Myth #3: You can't be harmed by these substances.
Fact: When prescribed for patients with ADHD and used correctly, prescription stimulants like Adderall or Ritalin are safe and helpful. However, the same medications can be harmful when taken by someone without ADHD.

Without a valid medical basis, stimulants can impair brain transmission. They can elevate your blood pressure, heart rate, and body temperature when used improperly or excessively, resulting in mood fluctuations, sleep loss, and other negative effects.

Myth #4: Occasionally, using someone else's prescription is acceptable.
Fact: Your weight, symptoms, and body chemistry are considered when prescribing medication. Doctors may change your drug or adjust your dosage to treat symptoms or address adverse effects.

You haven't been examined by a doctor when taking stimulants prescribed by a friend or family member. You could get sick from the potential adverse effects, and high blood pressure, lightheadedness, and fainting are all undesirable side effects.

Heart attacks and strokes are considerably worse. Depression and fatigue are additional potential side effects.

Myth #5: It doesn't matter how you take medication if your doctor prescribes it.
Fact: Stimulants that your doctor recommends can help if you have been diagnosed with ADHD. However, always take the prescription as prescribed—neither more nor less.

Also, inform your doctor of anything that occurs at home or school. It can be risky to mix prescribed stimulants with other medicines or alcohol.

Additionally, avoid giving your prescription medication to friends or family members who are abusing prescription medications.

THE REALITY
People will always try to convince you otherwise, no matter what you believe. Everyone wants their view to be heard and has an opinion. When it comes to the rumors, lies, and conspiracy surrounding ADHD, nothing could be more accurate.

Whether or not your child has ADHD, I can assure you that it is a genuine condition, and because of all the public interest and scrutiny, it is at least real. Beyond that, though, ADHD reflects variations in the way each person's brain works and how they see the environment.

If I could leave you with just one thought today, I would like you to know that ADHD is misunderstood. People refer to it as a deficit, but it reflects variances in how a child perceives, organizes, prioritizes, and thinks about the world.

In conclusion, to succeed in school and life, a child with ADHD requires the appropriate skills, resources, support, and understanding. By dispelling these misconceptions, women with ADHD can receive quicker, more efficient treatment, resulting in a calmer, more focused life. Women who accept their ADHD as a life partner open the door to living one's highest aspirations.

Depending on who you question, you might hear contrasting and conflicting accounts concerning this hypothesis. If you take it at its value, it is nothing more than a means of explaining how some individuals without ADHD imitate the very symptoms many of us experience.

However, other people would argue that relying on this notion merely makes life more difficult for those who experience the signs of attention deficit disorder regularly.

The bottom line in this situation is that neither actual truth nor myth is associated with this viewpoint.

Sincerity is damned, and it's only a means of classifying who we are and how we might be influenced by and affected by the complicated demands we encounter daily. It also demonstrates the pervasiveness of the oversimplified notion that everyone is familiar with ADHD.

Do not let it worry you if you genuinely battle with ADHD, those of you who, despite your best efforts, can't focus or finish tasks.

Recognizing that you have distinct ADHD symptoms that necessitate additional assistance and care in your life is crucial because you are also unique in all other respects.

It's harmless to you if you don't have the condition and think that everyone occasionally exhibits symptoms of ADHD. But remember that there are actual persons who have attention deficit disorder daily.

ADHD BRAIN VS. NORMAL BRAIN

If your child has ADHD, you are aware of the challenges they encounter compared to kids with brains that do not have the disorder. Due to this disorder, your child may struggle to focus, maintain stillness, or rein in impulsive activities.

Children with ADHD can be just as intelligent as those without it, but it might impact their behavior or performance in class and other crucial areas. Experts have discovered differences between the brains of those with and without the illness, which could alter as the youngster matures and develops.

DIFFERENCES BETWEEN AN ADHD BRAIN AND A BRAIN WITHOUT ADHD

Brain architecture in your youngster. According to certain research, people with ADHD may have smaller brain regions in some areas.

The lobes of your brain are distinct regions that each control a particular function. As its name suggests, your frontal lobe is at the front of your head. This area of your brain aids in the following:

- Organization
- Planning
- Focus
- Decision-making
- Problem-solving
- Memory
- Judgment
- impulse management
- Social behavior, Language, and Motivation
- Your capacity for postponing gratification
- The way you view time

Your child's frontal lobe may take longer to mature if they have ADHD than it would for someone without it. Certain brain regions that control emotional response and impulse control, which can be challenges for children with ADHD, were found to have reduced brain volumes in studies of adults with the disorder.

A decreased overall brain size may also be present in people with ADHD. Experts noted this more frequently in kids than in adults.

Your child's brain might not develop to the same level as people without ADHD since it has smaller, less developed areas.

The way your child's brain works. Changes in blood flow to specific regions of your child's brain, such as the prefrontal areas, may accompany ADHD, indicating that specific brain areas work less.

The high-level abilities that help you control your behaviors are known as executive functions, and the prefrontal region of your brain deals with them. These might have to do with your child's capacity for organization, planning, concentration, memory, and emotional responses.

According to experts, ADHD may inhibit certain parts of your brain from interacting properly. Functional brain connection is what they call it. According to one study, children with ADHD don't have the same brain connections as those without the disorder. The frontal cortex and the part of the brain responsible for visual processing may have distinct connections in an ADHD brain. This implies that individuals with ADHD may interpret information differently from those without the disorder.

The brain chemistry of your child. Your nerve cells communicate with the subsequent neuron, muscle, or gland cell through neurotransmitters, and your body uses them to process data from other organs. The neurotransmitters most closely linked to executive function—a common issue for those with ADHD—are dopamine and noradrenaline.

Your child's dopamine system is out of balance if they have ADHD. There might not be enough dopamine or dopamine receptors in them; however, their body could not utilize their dopamine properly.

Due to the symptoms of ADHD, doctors frequently recommend stimulant drugs. These medications may increase dopamine production or improve dopamine utilization in your child.

According to the medical world, attention deficit hyperactivity disorder is a biological ailment brought on by abnormalities in the brain, more specifically, a shortage of important neurotransmitters. Although the brains of persons with and without ADHD differ somewhat from one another, these variances are not the main reason for the disorder. Numerous environmental circumstances can cause ADHD to flare up, and imbalances in the ADHD brain are manifestations of the disorder's underlying causes.

In addition to functional differences in how their brains function, persons with ADD and those without it have several anatomical differences in their real brains. And many scientists and doctors are spending a lot of time and money figuring out these distinctions and writing about them. It doesn't mean their research doesn't exist or isn't real just because it's not interesting enough to be included on the Morning Show on television.

Studies using EEGs, Q-EEGs, CPTs, psychological testing, and "functional" MRIs are among the functional differences (fMRI). They revealed variations in the levels of brain activity in different regions, variations in brainwave patterns, and variations in glucose metabolism (as a proxy for the workload of the brain) between ADHD patients and controls. Additionally, they demonstrated that the ADD ADHD groups performed worse than the controls on timed activities, had longer response times, slower processing speeds, weaker problem-solving skills, less fine motor control, less gross motor control, different evoked potentials, and issues with inhibition. MRI, PET, and SPECT scan tests are part of the structural differences. The prefrontal cortex (smaller right anterior frontal cortex and less white matter in the right frontal lobes, which lead to difficulties with sustained or focused attention), caudate nucleus (asymmetries that lead to self-control), and globus pallidus all exhibit subtle structural differences. They also demonstrate that, on average, the right hemisphere of the ADHD brain is 5% smaller than that of the control groups. Additionally, they reveal specific chemical abnormalities in ADHD patients and variations in blood flow in particular brain regions.

It's fascinating to look at studies comparing the levels of essential fatty acids in ADHD vs. non-ADHD participants. Key essential fatty acid concentrations were significantly lower in the ADHD groups than in the control groups. Nearly 40% of the ADHD group displayed symptoms of EFA deficit (increased thirst, frequent urination, dry skin, and dry hair). Deficits in Omega 3 EFAs related to issues with learning, behavior, sleep, and temper, while low levels of Omega 6 EFAs increased the frequency of illness (colds, flu, etc.). These data bolster the argument for EFA supplementation as a component of an all-encompassing ADHD therapy strategy.

Gene changes have been linked to ADHD in some youngsters, according to genetic studies. They are paying close attention to the gene for the dopamine receptor DRD4. According to studies on familial genetics, attention deficit disorder occurs in families. For instance, a youngster who has an older sibling with ADHD is 300–500% more likely than a child without ADHD siblings to have ADHD themselves. Studies on twins and adoption are also included.

HOW IS A BRAIN WITH ADHD DIFFERENT FROM ONE WITHOUT?

Dopamine and norepinephrine, two neurotransmitters lacking in the ADHD brain, are likely to be mentioned by a medical professional. Neurotransmitters are the substances that convey messages between brain cells; when there are insufficient amounts, the brain cannot work at its best, resulting in persistent hyperactivity, impulsivity, and inattention. To correct the imbalance, doctors would likely prescribe drugs that stimulate brain circuits and momentarily raise dopamine levels, improving cognition, productivity, and conduct. The difference in the ADHD brain, however, is not primarily caused by a deficiency in neurotransmitters but rather by an issue with the electrical impulses required to release the neurotransmitters, according to the most recent studies on the brain anatomy of ADHD youngsters.

Alternative healthcare professionals look beyond the conventional diagnosis of ADHD, a neurotransmitter shortage, to identify three key variations in the ADHD brain. The most recent scientific findings support our knowledge of these three differences.

1. Hemisphere of the brain.

A healthy brain may easily engage both the left and right hemispheres. A person with ADHD, on the other hand, has a deficit in one of the two hemispheres. The right hemisphere is often weaker than the left, according to research.

2. A delay in brain circuitry development.

Brain hemispheric is typically a factor in developmental delays. This means that a child with ADHD may be ten years old chronologically, but some areas of their brain may be working at a level comparable to that of a six-year-old, which is why they have behavioral issues. Since complex contextual circumstances known as antecedents and triggers are the root cause of these developmental issues, the best treatment for ADHD should focus on removing these triggers rather than momentarily activating the brain with medications. The brain imbalance and symptoms will persist as long as antecedents and triggers continue to interact.

3. Sensory integration issues.

An individual with ADHD may experience difficulties processing sensory information because of brain hemispheric and developmental delay. Either they are overactive, or they are underactive (hypoactive). In either case, issues with sensory integration frequently result in behavioral issues.

Your child must undergo testing to identify any cognitive deficits before beginning an ADHD treatment program. Several experts can treat brain issues with secure methods like neurofeedback, sensory integration techniques, or chiropractic neurology. The best thing about these methods is that they are completely natural, so your child won't need to take any potentially harmful medications to address any potential brain deficiencies.

Keep in mind that a neurotransmitter imbalance is just one of the symptoms of ADHD, which is a condition brought on by a variety of environmental variables. Because of this, effective therapy for ADHD must address the environmental variables that cause the disorder in the first place, in addition to the brain.

The likelihood that both members of an identical twin pair will have ADHD is significantly higher than the likelihood for fraternal twins, even though ADHD is not inherited, like blond hair or blue eyes. This implies that the likelihood of a twin sharing a condition increases with the degree to which their genes are similar.

Additionally, research on brain activity has revealed that the frontal regions of the brain are underactive in children with ADHD. Since "hyperactivity" is typically associated with ADHD, this may seem strange. Yet frontal-lobe underactivity may indicate that these areas are not "keeping the lid on" disruptive behaviors, as the frontal regions of the brain have a soothing effect on more primitive regions.

THE ADHD BRAIN'S POORLY DEVELOPING

In a study at the National Institute of Mental Health, researchers used neuroanatomical magnetic resonance imaging to examine how the brains of children with ADHD and typically developing youngsters changed over time. Asymmetrical growth has previously been linked to normal motor and cognitive performance. The study's photos demonstrate that children with ADHD lack typical left-to-right brain asymmetry, with the prefrontal regions losing all asymmetry.

These results align with earlier brain imaging studies on ADHD kids that demonstrate a deficit in prefrontal brain control, which is known to be involved in attention. This latest study demonstrates that the issue arises during development, so it is essential to change the issue while the brain is still developing.

In the paradigm of mental health, a significant new element is emerging. One or more important brain parts cannot correctly generate functional connections when cognitive function challenges and various mental health disorders exist.

Brain inflammation is most likely the root of the issue. It may result from various factors, including chemicals in food, subpar food, GMO-modified food, pollution, stress, unstable environments, immunizations, epigenetic factors, and anything else that can cause an inflammatory state that can disrupt brain function and cause wear and tear to brain structure.

Positively, aerobic exercise is a significant brain structure regenerator. Anyone witheven a remotely dubious child should keep them active and devote a lot of time to sports, hobbies, crafts, and learning new physical abilities. These exercises encourage the growth of new neural connections. The key to solving this issue is consuming foods that support the development of healthy brain cells, the production of BDNF, and synaptic plasticity. DHA, pantethine, phosphatidylserine, magnesium, and blueberries are some nutrients.

The person will have a more stable brain as an adult if the ADHD condition, no matter how slight or major, can be adequately corrected throughout the brain's developmental years. Adults with problems can still improve, but it will take more time. This is a very different strategy from inducing attention in the brain using drugs that act like speed. These medications cause the brain to become more inflammatory and eventually burn out the structural integrity of the brain rather than creating connections.

THE REAL STORY OF ADHD, HYPERACTIVITY, AND THE DEVELOPING BRAIN

ADHD and hyperactivity go hand in hand like a glove. You'll learn in this article why excessive activity causes more issues than bad conduct and how to safely and naturally address and deal with it so your child may succeed at home and in school and have a happy, typical childhood.

HYPERACTIVITY, ADHD, AND THE DEVELOPING BRAIN

According to neuroscientists, "what fires together wires together." This indicates that the more often we engage in a particular activity, the more likely it is to persist in the future. The brain develops neural networks that support this behavior due to hyperactivity. The issue with this is that excessive activity puts the brain under stress, which impairs the capacity to focus and stay on task and may negatively impact development and the immune system. This is why it's so important to treat ADHD hyperactivity so that the brain may begin to repair itself and form new neural connections due to encounters with calm and focused mental states.

Drugs can treat ADHD and hyperactivity, but they come at a price. Every medicine has side effects, some of which can be very unsettling. For instance, appetite loss and sleeplessness are frequent adverse effects of ADHD medications. Your child's development will be stunted, and his symptoms may increase if he doesn't get enough food and sleep, making it much harder for him to function properly at home and school. Consider the long-term impacts on a developing brain before giving your child prescription medicines.

This is why so many parents use natural treatments to cure their kids. Natural cures don't have side effects like medications, and They won't interfere with any other medications your child might be prescribed.

FDA-approved high-quality natural remedies for treating hyperactivity and ADHD that contain substances like Hyoscyamus and Verta Alb have been shown in clinical testing to be beneficial. The best part is that natural treatments do more than just mask symptoms; they also mend the brain and reinstate normal function while calming and soothing the nervous system and improving focus. Refuse to allow your child's ADHD hyperactivity to persist into adulthood. Give your child a natural cure that will calm and mend the nervous system to prevent hyperactivity from becoming ingrained in the brain. This will allow your child to get back on track at home and school and experience a happy childhood.

CO-OCCURRING CONDITION IN ADHD

The followings are the signs and symptoms of ADHD that are most frequently experienced:

Acting without considering the effects, switching gears mid-task, being disorganized, and having the propensity to interject in other people's conversations are all impulsive.

Hyperactivity: a state of restlessness frequently characterized by restlessness, difficulty staying still, fidgeting, squirminess, and climbing on things.

Inattention includes being easily distracted, daydreaming, procrastinating on tasks, having trouble listening, and having clumsy motor skills.

It's also interesting to note that 30 to 50 percent of those with diagnoses continue to experience symptoms as adults. Adolescents and adults with ADHD will likely learn coping skills as they become older to compensate for their impairment.

ADHD does not account for sporadic bad behavior or discipline issues at school. Attention Deficit, Hyperactivity Disorder symptoms must be ongoing and present in various contexts, including family, school, and extracurricular activities.

A teacher, other parents, or nannies, for example, should be able to observe the signs or symptoms. Additionally, the behavior is out of character and is causing serious disruption. In other words, children might behave badly without having ADHD.

Two other points to be aware of are the hyperactivity's effects on others and the potential for harm, as well as the fact that circumstances like a family crisis or a significant shift in routine cannot account for the behavior.

A mix of excessive activity and short attention span, ADHD, or attention deficit hyperactivity disorder, frequently causes learning difficulties, social withdrawal, and isolation.

It is appropriate to speak with a physician who can assess your concerns, review the diagnostic standards, and provide referrals as necessary.

DISORDERS OF SLEEP AND ADHD

Does your child with ADHD sleep soundly, or do they wake up frequently during the night?

Everyone needs 7-9 hours of sleep each night to feel productive and well during the day. But people with ADHD often have a hard time falling or staying asleep.

Your ADHD symptoms worsen due to your fatigue, making it difficult for you to fall asleep the following night. This cycle continues. And many individuals experience it. According to one study, 67% of people with ADHD reported having trouble falling asleep or staying asleep.

Yet why? And what is the answer? Although scientists are unsure of the precise connection between sleep issues and ADHD, they know some potential causes and remedies.

Sleep issues can occur in children with ADHD, though they are not universal. About half of the parents in one study reported that their child with ADHD had trouble falling asleep. Parents mentioned that their kids had nightmares, felt exhausted when they woke up or suffered from other sleep issues, including sleep apnea or restless legs syndrome. Children with ADHD were found in another study to have less restorative sleep, trouble rising, and higher daytime sleepiness.

ADHD SLEEP ISSUES: CAUSES AND EFFECTS

If you have ADHD, there may be additional difficulties on top of the typical factors preventing anyone from getting a good night's sleep. These consist of the following:

Issues with following a schedule. People who have ADHD are frequently quickly distracted and struggle to put down tasks, ignore distractions, and fall asleep. Even once you are in bed, it might be challenging to unwind sufficiently to fall asleep.

Stimulants. You may feel more alert and find it difficult to fall asleep if you take the stimulant drugs commonly prescribed for ADHD. Additionally, you may consume caffeine through beverages, including coffee, tea, soda, and chocolate.

Other circumstances. People with ADHD may struggle to fall asleep due to anxiety, despair, mood disorders, or substance misuse.

LINKED SLEEP DISORDERS TO ADHD

Sleep disorders are more than just restless nights. And if you have one, it can prevent you from getting enough sleep and make you more impulsive and distracted during the day. Due to the prevalence of these illnesses among those with ADHD, professionals frequently include sleep issues when making an ADHD diagnosis.

The following are a few of the more typical sleep problems to look out for:

INSOMNIA.
People with ADHD are likely to experience insomnia for various reasons, including prescription side effects and difficulty adhering to a routine. At night, you can experience bursts of activity and racing thoughts that make it difficult to fall asleep. Even when you sleep, it might not be very restful, particularly if you also experience nightmares. Additionally, worrying about your insomnia can make it worse.

CIRCADIAN-RHYTHM SLEEPING PROBLEMS.
To adapt to the varying amounts of light and darkness over a 24-hour day, your body alters during the day. Your body may occasionally be out of sync with the cycle and fail to release hormones like melatonin when they should. In turn, that can make it challenging to get to sleep. Your body's internal clock can be disrupted by bright lights, especially artificial blue lights like laptops and tablets.

ADHD AND SNORING
At night, enlarged tonsils and adenoids may partially obstruct the airway. Poor sleep and snoring may result from this.

The following day, attention issues could result from that. Children with mild ADHD snored more frequently than normal children in a study of 5- to 7-year-olds. Another study found that children who snore had almost double the likelihood of having ADHD as their classmates. That did not, however, demonstrate that snoring caused ADHD.

Snoring kids typically perform lower on attention, language, and general IQ tests. According to some research, removing the tonsils and adenoids may improve behavior without requiring medication by promoting better sleep.

ADHD AND SLEEP APNEA
People with sleep apnea experience brief spells of not breathing, even when they are unaware of it. These incidents could often occur all through the night.

Enlarged tonsils and adenoids most frequently bring on children's cases of sleep apnea. But other factors include obesity and persistent allergies.

Children with sleep apnea will experience daytime fatigue similar to adults. They could have trouble concentrating and exhibit other sleep-related symptoms. For example, they might feel agitated.

Children with sleep apnea can be treated. If your child has tonsils that are large enough to potentially block the airway and result in sleep apnea, your pediatrician or an ear, nose, and throat specialist can examine your child.

The child might undergo a sleep study in a specialized facility to verify the diagnosis. Sleep apnea is not always present in children with enlarged tonsils or loud snoring.

The breathing of those with sleep apnea fluctuates throughout the night, disrupting your sleep and making you feel exhausted. 25% of people with ADHD and about 3% of the general suffer from sleep apnea or another "sleep-disordered breathing" issue. You might want to inform your doctor if you snore a lot because loud snoring can indicate this condition.

Surgery is the preferred action for children with enlarged tonsils and adenoids. Other treatments are available for those who experience difficulty breathing at night due to allergies or other conditions.

RESTLESS LEGS SYNDROME AND ADHD
Studies show links between sleep disruption and ADHD and restless legs syndrome (RLS) and ADHD. The legs and occasionally the arms experience a creeping, crawling sensation when one has restless legs syndrome. There is a strong want to move as a result of this experience. Sleep disturbances and daytime drowsiness are consequences of restless legs syndrome.

People who experience restless legs syndrome and the resulting sleep disruption may feel irritable, moody, or hyperactive, all of which can be signs of ADHD.

Leg pain and a strong impulse to move your legs while you sleep are symptoms. Inside your leg, the sensation is sometimes described as pulling, throbbing, aching, or itching. RLS affects 44% of people with ADHD and about 2% of all people.

According to some experts, some persons with ADHD and those with restless legs syndrome may share a dopamine-related issue. However, not all people with ADHD experience restless legs.

ADHD AND NARCOLEPSY
Some children with ADHD exhibit narcolepsy symptoms. There are several of these: extreme daytime sleepiness, rapid loss of muscle

tone brought on by intense emotions (cataplexy), hallucinations, and sleep paralysis.

About two times as many kids with narcolepsy also have ADHD. Research indicates that children with narcolepsy may struggle to manage their ADHD symptoms with medication.

STEPS YOU CAN TAKE

You should tell your doctor if you struggle with sleep because of ADHD. You might need to adjust your prescription to help you fall asleep, or you might have a sleep study to determine whether there is another underlying reason for your inability to sleep.

If all other potential explanations have been checked out, your ADHD symptoms may be to blame. By engaging in the healthy routines and practices listed below, you may be able to enhance your sleep. You ought to:

- Four hours before night, avoid taking a sleep.
- Caffeine should not be consumed four hours before bed.
- Make careful to take any stimulant medication you take as early as feasible.
- Establish a relaxing nighttime ritual.
- Set your alarm for roughly the same time every day.
- Sleep peacefully and quietly in a cozy bed.
- Avoid using screens and electronic media in the evening, including TVs, smartphones, and other devices.

SUPPORT YOUR CHILD'S ADHD

Get enough rest.

Be a "caffeine-free" household. Keep an eye out for caffeine in your child's food.

Keep coffee and other caffeinated items out of the kitchen.

Be dependable. Have a regular daily schedule that includes set bedtimes, waking times, mealtimes, and family time.

Block out the noise. Use a "white noise" machine that produces a humming sound if your child is bothered by noises while sleeping. Get earplugs for kids who are extra sensitive to noise.

When your child is sleeping, keep the room dark. Melatonin generation by the body can be hampered by exposure to light.

Avoid using sleep aids. Please consult your child's doctor before administering any medication unless it is essential.

Think about the medical issues. Asthma, allergies, or other painful illnesses may cause sleep disturbances. Consult your doctor if your child has trouble breathing or snores loudly. Sleep issues can also be a sign of despair and anxiety.

Make sure your child exercises every day. Avoid working out shortly before bed. According to studies, daily exercise promotes restful sleep.

Before bedtime, give your youngster a warm bath. Sleep often occurs after the body's temperature cycle's cooling phase. Keep your child's bedroom temperature cool after a bath to see if that helps.

Before bed, please avoid TV, violent video games, and roughhousing, as it's too energizing.

Examine your child's prescriptions. Inform your doctor about your child's sleep issues. A shorter-acting medicine may be helpful, so ask your doctor if you can take the morning dose of your ADHD medication earlier in the day.

ADHD AND DEPRESSION: A CONNECTION

Depression and attention deficit hyperactivity disorder (ADHD) frequently coexist. They can coexist together and are sometimes referred to as comorbid or coexisting conditions by doctors.

The neurological condition of ADHD makes it challenging to concentrate. It can make it difficult for kids and adults to accomplish chores, sit still, or remember things like appointments or details.

Depression is more than just a passing mood swing. You experience extreme melancholy and despair every day for at least two weeks, and it could be challenging to work, study, or sleep.

Around 30% of kids with ADSHD also suffer from severe mood illnesses like depression. More than half of those with the illness will need therapy for depression at some time in their lives, according to some specialists.

WHAT'S THE RELATIONSHIP?

It might be challenging to detect and handle depression and ADHD because they share many symptoms. For instance, the inability to concentrate is a symptom of melancholy and ADHD. Additionally, medications for ADHD symptoms may interfere with your sleep or eating patterns, both of which can be indicators of depression. Hyperactivity and irritability in kids might be signs of melancholy in addition to ADHD.

Additionally, when persons with ADHD struggle with their symptoms, it can cause depression. Adults may experience problems at work, while kids may struggle at school or with playmates. Deep feelings of hopelessness and other symptoms of depression may result from that.

Both conditions appear to be related to your family history. However, doctors are unsure what causes either one. A parent or other family member frequently suffers from depression or ADHD.

ADHD AND DEPRESSION TREATMENT

Both diseases are often treated with a combination of medication and therapy sessions.

What condition is giving you the most trouble may determine how you begin. For instance, if ADHD contributes to stress, treating it first may help remove one of the factors contributing to depression.

Stimulants that increase the brain's focus- and thinking-related neurotransmitters are frequently used to treat ADHD. They can assist with symptoms while you're at work or school but also reduce your appetite, give you headaches, or interfere with sleep.

Some ADHD medications don't include stimulants and don't have the same adverse effects as stimulants. Yet they might not function as rapidly.

Your doctor might prescribe a mix of stimulant and non-stimulant medications.

Your doctor may recommend antidepressants to treat depression. These may have negative effects, such as suicidal thoughts, and require many weeks to start working. While taking them, parents should keep a watchful eye on kids, especially teenagers.

In addition to stimulants, antidepressants may be used to treat the symptoms of ADHD alone or in conjunction with other medications to treat both diseases.

How to control your symptoms and lead a healthy life might be discussed in psychotherapy. A therapist can provide coping mechanisms for common problems, such as problems with friends, family, work, or school.

THE NEGATIVE EFFECT OF ADHD, IF NOT TREATED

A brain-based disorder, ADHD may obstruct your child's regular home and school activities. Children that have it sometimes become hyperactive and have difficulty managing their behavior and paying attention.

It will help if you note your child's symptoms before diagnosing them. You can keep tabs on them with the CDC's checklist for kids with ADHD.ss

The warning indicators are as follows:

Disorganization, difficulty keeping focused, persistent daydreaming, and failure to pay attention when spoken to directly are all examples of inattention.

Impulsivity: Includes making snap judgments without considering the potential for harm or long-term consequences. They take swift action to get an immediate benefit. They might frequently scold classmates, friends, and relatives.

Squirming, tapping, chatting, and frequent movement are all examples of hyperactivity, especially in inappropriate settings.

Teens with ADHD are especially at risk when they drive. They are two to four times more likely than teens without ADHD to be involved in an automobile accident.

Teens who have ADHD may be impulsive, reckless, judgmentally immature, and thrill-seeking. These characteristics increase the likelihood of accidents and severe injuries.

However, research indicates that teenagers with ADHD who take medication have a lower accident rate.

Those with ADHD are more likely than teens without ADHD to be heavy drinkers. Additionally, they are more susceptible to drinking-related issues.

According to studies, kids with ADHD were three times more likely to abuse drugs besides marijuana and twice as likely to have abused alcohol in the preceding six months than other teens.

The likelihood of eventual alcohol and drug dependence may be reduced with the appropriate therapy for ADHD.

Talk to your teen about driving privileges in the context of their overall ADHD treatment plan. Establishing guidelines and expectations for safe driving conduct is your duty. Include a discussion on the dangers of texting and talking on the phone while operating a vehicle.

CHALLENGES TO FAMILY NORMS AND BELIEFS DUE TO ATTENTION DEFICIT HYPERACTIVITY DISORDER (ADHD)

The most prevalent behavioral disorder in children is Attention Deficit Hyperactivity Disorder (ADHD). Between 3% and 6% of children and adolescents in the US are thought to have ADHD, according to estimates. According to a recent American Psychiatric Association (APA) report, however, as many as 8% to 17% of American children and adolescents may be affected by ADHD. According to the APA assessment, there is a bigger hazard to public health than previously believed.

Children and teenagers with ADHD are much more likely than those without it to have a wide range of emotional and social issues, including academic and professional underachievement, violence and crime, an increase in suicide attempts, and risk-taking behavior. Additionally, melancholy, interpersonal issues, and family instability are risks for children with ADHD.

Even though studies have shown that families with children with ADHD frequently experience family problems, and family members may also have major psychological repercussions. Still, there is a clear absence of understanding regarding how to assist these families in coping with the difficulties ADHD presents daily.

Most professionals recognize ADHD as a medical disorder, and I can't entirely agree with that conclusion. True, there is a medical and physiological aspect to ADHD. But in my opinion, ADHD is a psychological, behavioral, and physiological condition. We run the danger of only treating a portion of the symptoms when we treat ADHD as a single entity. For instance, if we concentrate on the medical part of ADHD, the doctor is frequently consulted to assess whether the child satisfies the DSM-IV-TR criteria for ADHD (DSM IV). The evaluating doctors are also consulted for guidance and to recommend a course of treatment for the illness. The majority of doctors, however, have highly busy practices and are unable to spend the time necessary with the family discussing the nature and causes of ADHD as well as the multidisciplinary approach to treating the illness. There is a high chance that the doctor would unintentionally confirm family members' preexisting anxieties and beliefs regarding ADHD.

In light of this, it is clear how important the multidisciplinary team's interactions with and support of families during the interviewing and consultation processes were. According to research, a child's family may directly impact how parents feel about their children and how they interact with them. It is a well-known fact that how parents react to the news depends on the information they receive, how sympathetically they are treated, and how attentively the doctor and other experts deliver the message. This road map can support families through the procedure and aid the team in developing a plan to lessen family members' anxieties.

Due to the increased focus on ADHD in the media, many members of the general population have opinions about the disorder that are not based on scientific evidence.

Is ADD or ADHD Real?
Some members of the medical profession deviated from science and invented a condition by regularly giving kids drugs to make them behave properly to ease the concerns of teachers and parents about children's inappropriate behavior. A deluge of scientific studies and research material that establishes ADHD as a real and serious condition must be ignored by those who still think it is medical fiction. Compared to all other psychiatric and behavioral issues of children and adolescents, ADHD receives the most referrals to child mental health clinics, according to the DSM IV criteria.

Many physicians and the general public have doubts regarding the therapy of ADHD due to the ongoing debate over the accuracy of the diagnosis. It may be difficult for certain patients to receive the proper care and be unclear about the requirement for an approved course of therapy due to inaccurate ideas about ADHD. As was already mentioned, detractors claim that ADHD is a designation given to troubled kids whose behavior is the issue rather than their health. They further claim that ADHD doesn't have a biological basis and is instead the product of poor parenting and ineffective educational methods. These viewpoints add to the stigmatization of patients and their families and the burden of this crippling illness. There is abundant medical evidence that ADHD not only results in a specific set of incapacitating symptoms that frequently last into adulthood, but there is also a biological basis for it and that it responds in a particular way to recognized treatments.

The renowned actor and comedian Rodney Dangerfield frequently said, "I get no respect." My first thought was that ADHD is not respected. After reading so many false claims that ADHD is not a real, severe condition, that is undoubtedly the conclusion one may draw. Many of us who work with children diagnosed with ADHD, including this author, are fully aware of the severity and reality of this illness.

Today's educational environments put me in regular touch with pupils who have been identified as having various disorders, including ADHD. I also harbor a deep hatred toward individuals who uphold the notion that ADHD is merely a moniker invented to relieve parents and educators of their duty to regulate unruly children and not a real medical condition. I do, however, recognize how easily misinformed individuals and those who observe ADHD from a distance could be misled.

For instance, many of us have displayed some signs of ADHD at some point. We occasionally become preoccupied, which causes us to struggle with completing homework assignments or other crucial chores. On the other side, kids with ADHD are typically less able to take care of themselves, act correctly in social situations, and communicate on par with other kids their age.

PHANTOM SIGNS

Last but not least, for an unexplained cause, symptoms of ADHD may momentarily disappear, leading others to believe that the person with ADHD has behavioral control. A definitive diagnosis is also challenging because there are no reliable tests to identify ADHD. Only after seeing the child's behavior can a doctor determine whether or not the child has ADHD. On the day they visit the doctor, if a youngster has problems paying attention or seems disobedient, this could result in an inaccurate diagnosis. As a result, ADHD must be identified by medical specialists with expertise in these illnesses, the assistance, and participation of parents and teachers

PART TWO: ADHD IN WOMEN

There is little information on how attention deficit hyperactivity disorder (ADHD) specifically affects adult women. The subjects of study are more frequently men, children, and teenagers. Studies, even in young toddlers, reveal that guys are diagnosed correctly more frequently than girls.

These disparities may be caused by gender bias and underappreciated ADHD symptoms. Compared to boys, girls typically exhibit less "hyperactive" behavior. Most research tends to concentrate heavily on the hyperactive ADHD characteristics that are more prevalent in guys. ADHD symptoms in young females who are not treated may worsen into adulthood. ADHD can lower your overall quality of life if it is not treated.

HISTORICAL PERSPECTIVES ON WOMEN'S ADHD

The way we comprehend ADHD has substantially changed. ADHD, which was once thought only to be characterized by measurements of hyperactivity in children, is now recognized to include inattentiveness and can last a lifetime. Even so, many antiquated ADHD assumptions exist, both inside and outside the medical profession, making it difficult to study, identify, and treat ADHD in women today. According to a recent study, women who are improperly diagnosed and treated for ADHD due to harmful beliefs like the following are likely to suffer from substantial mental and physical health consequences:

It is a masculine disorder, ADHD. Boys who were considered to be rowdy and unruly and who were hyperactive were referred to clinics. Early research was centered on the actions of these hyperactive white boys, and the conclusions from these investigations influenced the diagnostic standards and assessment tools still in use today. A childhood disorder is ADHD. Based on its defining characteristic of hyperactivity, ADHD has long been categorized as a Disruptive Behavior Disorder of Childhood. It has become increasingly obvious that ADHD symptoms do not go away with puberty and that inattentive symptoms last longer than hyperactive ones.

HOW TO KNOW IF A WOMAN HAS ADHD

Most female ADHD sufferers receive a precise diagnosis in their late 30s or 40s. According to experts, there could be several causes for the delayed diagnosis.

Young girls' ADHD symptoms and behaviors may go unnoticed by parents, teachers, or pediatricians because they aren't immediately noticeable. Additionally, clinicians likely misdiagnose adolescents and young women with ADHD in favor of other mood disorders like anxiety or despair. Additionally, some recent studies indicate that women may have signs of ADHD later in life. To prove it, however, scientists contend that more study is necessary.

Adult females may exhibit the following symptoms and indicators of ADHD:
- Difficulty managing one's time
- Disorganization
- I'm feeling overpowered
- anxiety and despair in the past
- difficulty managing finances

ADHD may run in families. If your child or sibling is diagnosed with ADHD, you are more likely to become aware of your symptoms if you have undiagnosed ADHD. Additionally, it's not unusual for women with ADHD to struggle with concurrent issues like compulsive overeating, persistent sleep deprivation, or excessive alcohol consumption.

Women who have ADHD are more likely to experience the following:

The DSM-5 lists several inattentive symptom presentations, such as failing to pay close attention to details or engaging in thoughtless behavior.
- difficulty focusing on activities, difficulty carrying out instructions, and failure to complete tasks (e.g., losing focus, getting sidetracked)
- arranging duties and activities is difficult,
- and prone to distraction, forgetfulness during regular tasks,and internalization of symptoms, such as depression and anxiety.

Women with ADHD may present as timid, introverted, withdrawn, and daydreamers who are frequently disorganized, perplexed, or overwhelmed. It can also be perceived as a person who is impulsive, moody, overly social, hyperactive, and chatty. ADHD symptoms are amplified when combined with the fluctuating hormones experienced by a teen or adult with premenstrual syndrome. The difficulties these girls and women may face are emotional instability, impatience, and mood swings.

Understanding and managing the socioeconomic concerns that most women deal with daily gets more challenging. For instance, a married woman who is expected to care for and maintain her home could feel unqualified. Even though she might not have a support system or a confidante, she has persisted in being everyone else's supporter. An already overburdened person is under further pressure and stress by managing a full-time job and full-time responsibilities at home. The abovementioned challenges lower their self-esteem, contribute to despair and anxiety, and worsen any problems that ADHD may already be causing in their lives.

HOW DOES WOMEN'S ADHD APPEAR?

Many doctors continue to make mistakes. What does female ADHD look like? Common symptoms of undiagnosed ADHD in women include depressive moods and persistent anxiety, which clinicians frequently misinterpret and misdiagnose.

Michelle, a 38-year-old mother of two, told her internist, "I'm almost at the end of my rope." "I leave our flat and come back three times to get whatever I forgot. I don't make meal plans and cannot attend school meetings, health appointments, or sporting events. I'm having trouble sleeping and am always worried that I won't be able to go through my day without anything going wrong.

Her internist told her, "Michelle, you're depressed and nervous." She gave him a prescription for an antidepressant called a selective serotonin reuptake inhibitor (SSRI).

Michelle left the doctor's office feeling heard and satisfied with a reasonable diagnosis and treatment strategy. Except for the fact that it was incorrect. Misinterpreted and incorrectly classified as symptoms of melancholy or anxiety, Michelle's frustration, worry, underachievement, depressive moods, and chronic anxiety were indicators of women's ADHD.

WHY CLINICIANS IGNORE WOMEN'S ADHD

Many women with inattentive signs of ADHD experience what occurred to Michelle, a fictional character. The majority of specialists, including psychologists and medical physicians, have limited training in ADHD and are unable to identify it in people who are not hyperactive youngsters. People with inattentive ADHD describe anxiety and depressive feelings due to their struggles to reach their goals (because they fear dropping the many balls they are juggling).

The prescription seems appropriate because all strip doctors know that SSRIs effectively treat depression and anxiety. These undiagnosed ADHD women are primarily "depressed" because they perform below par, lag, and feel humiliated. They experience "anxiety" since they never know what negative event will occur next, and SSRIs won't assist with this.

IMPACT OF ADHD ON WOMEN

Do specific times of the month make your ADHD symptoms worse? Do you tend to be more productive and organized the week following your period but forgetful the week before? The severity of ADHD symptoms and hormonal changes appear to be related, according to experts on the disorder. The effects of hormones on ADHD can continue for a lifetime; they are not just cyclical. A female adult's typical age at which they receive an ADHD diagnosis ranges from 36 to 38.

Hormonal changes are rarely taken into account by medical professionals who assess women for ADHD when developing a treatment plan. But this is beginning to change as more people become aware of ADHD and the impact of hormones.

The four main stages of a woman's life, the hormonal changes that occur throughout these times, and the most effective techniques to treat symptoms are listed below.

1. **ADOLESCENCE**

The female body produces more estrogen and progesterone, the sex hormones, during puberty. These "raging hormones" frequently result in risky behavior, disobedience, and heightened impulsivity. Girls with ADHD are likely to struggle academically, try drugs, and act aggressively during their early adolescent years. Watch for indications that your daughter's symptoms are getting worse so you can assist her. Encourage her to complete activities, prepare for a large test, or start a paper a week in advance when you observe this happening. Determine her assets and emphasize them when she is going through a particularly trying time emotionally. If she starts to argue, try to be patient with her; rather than yelling, offer her a better approach to handle the matter.

2. **THE YEARS OF CHILDBEARING**

Estrogen levels increase throughout the first two weeks of the menstrual cycle. Dopamine and serotonin are released by this hormone, which explains why women are more adept at controlling their ADHD symptoms at this time of the cycle. Progesterone levels rise in the third and fourth weeks and begin to counteract the advantages of estrogen. According to experts, women with ADHD are more likely than those without to experience severe premenstrual syndrome (PMS). The good news is that PMS can be cured of ADHD with the correct care.

3. **PREGNANCY AND CHILDBIRTH**

During pregnancy, hormones fluctuate. In addition to producing additional hormones, the placenta also induces the thyroid and adrenal glands to create more hormones. Expectant mothers with ADHD are more likely to feel anxiety, mood fluctuations, and exhaustion during the first few months of pregnancy. The good news is that these symptoms improve as the pregnancy progresses. Hormone levels fall after childbirth, which can lead to postpartum depression or mood changes. Verify that any medication you are taking for ADHD is safe while nursing or pregnant.

4. **MENOPAUSE**

You would have seen a 65% decrease in estrogen levels during menopause or your final menstruation. This hormone decline happens gradually during the perimenopause, or the ten years preceding menopause, rather than abruptly. Compared to women without ADHD, perimenopausal women with ADHD frequently experience fatigue, memory loss, irritability, and moodiness. Look for natural remedies to balance your hormones, like consuming foods high in phytoestrogens (plant estrogens). Additionally, exercise frequently. While hormone replacement therapy may seem alluring, it may result in a hormonal imbalance that worsens the consequences of perimenopause and makes your ADHD symptoms worse.

A MOTHER'S TALE

Rachael, a 26-year-old mother of three from Sandy, Utah, battled anxiety and despair for years without understanding why. She overreacted to everything that went wrong in her life.

Hall, a client of Reimherr's, recalls her honeymoon breakdown due to difficulty understanding a set of driving instructions: "I told my husband, 'Why don't you leave me? I am nothing. Just one tiny thing would become out of hand. Following that, I would begin to feel bad, and the more guilty I felt, the more unhappy I felt.

Even worse for Hall were the strains of parenthood. She broke down and was admitted to the hospital for depression while she was carrying her third kid. Doctors prescribed antidepressants. She claims, "It didn't work at all." It appeared as though I was careless, and it removed everything. I didn't experience joy, and I had no sense of sadness.

Following the birth of her daughter, Hall started having frequent angry outbursts. She explains, "I would be fine one second and a roaring banshee the next." "I was a jerk to the people I loved, and I could not continue.

Hall speculated that the woman might be experiencing postpartum depression. However, her doctor disqualified it, stating that it had been too long since her due date for that to be a possibility.

One day, Hall found a research ad for mood problems at Reimherr's clinic. She chose to sign up.

She remembers, "I got frustrated at first." "I must be on a placebo because it's not working," I said to my spouse. I then observed a difference as soon as the second five weeks began.

She was taking Concerta, an ADHD medication, but she was unaware of this during the second five weeks. She appeared to think "more logically" due to the drug. She was less irritable and forgetful. She claims, "I'm generally in a better mood. "I am joyful. I don't exaggerate anything, in my opinion.

Hall's relationship with her family has improved since she kept up her treatment, and she no longer experiences social anxiety. She describes herself as the lively, talkative, center-of-attention type. I'm outgoing, but not to the point where I'd make a fool of myself. Now I can draw attention to myself, be witty, and win people over, but not to the point where I annoy them.

Hall's experience is not unusual. There is a deeply entrenched social expectation for women to be self-controlled and organized and to be the one who keeps everyone else organized. Women feel like failures if they can't keep their houses in order. It costs a lot to maintain appearances, struggle, and experience uncomfortable situations. Explicit statements such as, "I forgot to pick up my kids after soccer practice, and they were the only ones left standing outside." It's a public failing; women frequently don't get pardoned for this behavior. They'll remark about a man, "Oh, he's so busy, of course, he forgot.

It might be challenging for women to deal with the perception that they are "different" from their peers.

She can have worry, sadness, low self-esteem, and a gloomy appearance. She is uncomfortably aware, then. She truly suffers, but she keeps quiet about it.

Aside from the emotional difficulties, ADHD may also have a substantial financial impact.

You continuously pay for your disorganization and carelessness. "You must buy new spectacles since you keep losing your current ones. Since you lost track of time and the meter ran out, you received a parking charge. That sort of thing could frequently occur in the life of an ADHD person.

Mother of three, Lyle Hawkins, 59, had long suspected she had ADHD but wasn't identified or treated until she was 40. She laments all those years of being misperceived as lazy and thoughtless. But most of all, she laments wasted opportunities. Hawkins got married right out of high school, but she believes she probably would have attended college if she had had an early diagnosis and treatment that worked.

Hawkins, a patient of Dr. Reimherr from Sandy, Utah, says, "I was from an educated family, where knowledge was essential." But going to college would have been too demanding. Everyone is on page 10, while you're on page three when you have attention deficit disorder.

The medical profession is beginning to recognize that ADHD is a significant issue for girls and that it frequently lasts into adulthood. For the time being, any woman who believes she may have ADHD should learn more about the disorder and speak with a mentalhealth expert who specializes in the area.

A doctor's credentials are less important than their knowledge of and experience treating ADHD in women.

Many women feel that their general practitioner can be helpful if he addresses ADHD in older teenagers. "A therapist or psychiatrist is typically most qualified to diagnose the illness in women.

It makes it reasonable for a doctor to identify a lady as depressed and treat her for it if she is depressed. However, it may also make sense to question the diagnosis and to keep doing so until she receives relief for her symptoms if she has cause to feel that there is more to her issue (or if procrastination, time management issues, or forgetfulness remains despite therapy for depression).

Women are adept at making the most of their newly acquired knowledge, even when the diagnosis occurs later in life. The mother of three and 59-year-old Lyle Hawkins observed many of her ADHD characteristics in her kids. Hawkins ensured they received an early diagnosis because she didn't want them to experience the same thing. She claims they would have slipped through the cracks if I hadn't been their mother.

WHAT CAUSES ADHD IN WOMEN

Interestingly, many women with ADHD have survived into adulthood without ever receiving a diagnosis. In many cases, adult females don't become aware that they exhibit some of these ADHD symptoms until their children have been diagnosed.

Due to these ADHD characteristics, the woman would appear disorganized, excessively indecisive, forgetful, and self-absorbed. Additionally, it is not unusual for a woman with ADHD to live until adulthood without ever receiving a diagnosis. If you are disturbed that you or a loved one has the disease, here are some additional and more prevalent signs of being aware of.

- Focusing issues - Women with ADHD have trouble focusing on tasks for extended periods.
- Emotional sensitivity - women with ADHD often become angry easily since they are very emotional and sensitive to criticism.
- Habitual tardiness - One of the ADHD symptoms that affect women more frequently is their bad sense of time, which is demonstrated by the fact that they frequently arrive late for appointments and work.
- Hyper-focusing - While ADHD is often linked with the lack or difficulty of paying attention for extended periods, women with the illness frequently exhibit hyper-focus on projects and achieve outstanding outcomes.
- Hypersensitivity concerns - many ADHD-affected women have overwhelming feelings in crowded spaces and are overly sensitive to sounds, scents, and tastes.
- Inability to complete projects - Women with ADHD symptoms frequently find it difficult to accomplish projects because they easily become overwhelmed and have trouble organizing their work.
- Lower self-esteem - women frequently experience failures in their lives that go back to their early years, which causes them to grow to have lower self-esteem.
- Social issues - many women with the illness find it difficult to connect with and communicate with others. Therefore they make snap decisions like forgetting people's names or tuning them out when speaking.
- Organizational difficulties - women with ADHD will struggle to organize their living and working spaces and will make piles of various items to achieve organization.

- Finally, sleep problems are another ADHD sign affecting women rather frequently. Women with ADHD have trouble falling asleep or staying asleep all night since they move around a lot, which makes most people quite fatigued.
- Last but not least, you should schedule a test with your family doctor if you believe you or a loved one may have Attention Deficit Disorder and exhibit ADHD symptoms. There are numerous treatment options, some of which exclude medicine use.

Regarding ADHD, girls and women are frequently underdiagnosed or incorrectly diagnosed.

It can be because they've mastered disguising or adjusting for their symptoms. Alternately, health experts, educators, and parents may be less likely to notice signs of inattention than they are to notice louder, more intrusive symptoms.

Moreover, women are more prone to:
- Symptom changes brought on by hormone fluctuations
- Because of their ADHD, they develop depression and anxiety disorders, have reduced self-esteem, and have more relationship difficulty.

Women with ADHD might anticipate treatments that work better for them as unique individuals as more research focuses on the lived experiences of women with ADHD.

Here's something to think about for the moment.

You are not a slacker if you have ADHD and are not a bumbling idiot. You have a mental health issue that makes it difficult or occasionally impossible to pay attention, control impulses, plan, organize, and complete tasks, like the 4.4 percent of adults in the United States described by NIMH

Proper medical care might be likened to turning a tapestry on its artistic side. The tangle of threads and knots can start to make stunning, vibrant sense. Women with ADHD

ADHD or ADD affects people of all genders equally. The majority of children with ADHD never outgrow their symptoms, and they appear almost as frequently in females as they do in boys. Additionally, evidence from science strongly supports that ADHD is inherited. This indicates that there is a good probability you have ADHD if you are the mother of a child who struggles with attention and impulsivity.

Most women are shocked by this discovery since they have always believed that hyperactive boys are the only ones with ADHD, and it's not. Adult ADHD is a legitimate condition, and women can also have ADHD.

RISK FACTORS FOR WOMEN WITH ADHD

Compared to males with ADHD, women with ADHD frequently have increased central nervous system sensitivity. More frequently, they report the following:
- defensive tactual behavior
- somatic problems, such as nausea, stomach aches, headaches, and migraines
- issues with sleep

By adulthood, most women with ADHD have at least one comorbid disorder, which can exacerbate the symptoms of ADHD.
- anxiety (Anxiety disorders are present in 25–40% of patients with ADHD)
- mood problems
- uncontrolled eating (bulimia is most common)
- externalizing disorders such as conduct disorder or oppositional defiant disorder (mostly found in women with impulsive-type ADHD)
- a borderline personality disorder is one example of a personality disorder (BPD)

Impulsivity signs also have an impact on how ADHD manifests in females. Impulsivity has a connection to
Behaviors viewed as controlling, demanding, easily agitated, etc., are examples of gender atypical behaviors.
A much higher likelihood of acting on negative feelings, including self-harm, is associated with high-risk behaviors like speeding and extreme sports and addictive behaviors like substance use and gambling (picking skin, cutting, etc.)

IS YOUR CHILD AT RISK FOR VIOLENT BEHAVIOR RELATED TO ADHD?

Whether or not your ADHD child exhibits this type of rage and violence, you should be aware that it is potential with every ADHD child. You may hear a lot on the news about violent behavior associated with ADHD. While ADHD does not always result in aggressive behavior, its symptoms can lead to tantrums, screaming, or even physical violence long after kids have reached an age when they should be able to regulate these behaviors. Here is what you should know about violent behavior in children with ADHD if you are the child's caregiver:

1. While not all children with ADHD are violent, their shortened attention spans can make them more likely to become impatient when they have to wait or figure things out. These irritations might trigger violent behavior in children with ADHD if they aren't properly handled early.
2. Irritability is the simplest form of anger that ADHD can impact. ADHD children can grow irrational enough to have tantrums well past the proper developmental period for such outbursts, which is between 18 months and three years old. This is because they are more easily upset than most kids.
3. If parents or other caregivers give in to the child's tantrums, the child will develop a pattern of learned rage. Once he realizes that acting irrationally will get him what he wants, he will keep using his anger against you. The only way to stop this cycle—or prevent it from starting in the first place—is to persistently maintain your composure in the face of a child's tantrums. You may find this challenging and annoying, but the outcome will be beneficial.
4. Rage behavior is the most severe form of aggressive ADHD behavior. Things can become deadly at this point, especially for older ADHD kids. Numerous factors can contribute to rage behavior, but ADHD-related impulsivity is to blame at its core. Rage behavior might include violent outbursts and physical abuse, but it's not something kids intentionally do. His impulsive side takes over when he is furious and loses control of his actions, which may entail harming himself or other people.

Ritalin and Adderall are examples of traditional drugs that may help reduce some symptoms of ADHD child violence, but they can also have some very dangerous adverse effects. After discussing rage behavior, the most concerning sign is that when a child has been taking medicine for a time and changes dosages or stops taking medication entirely, his violence might escalate enormously.

Children with ADHD who are violent may respond better to homeopathic medications. These plant- and herb-based remedies can restore a child's brain chemistry, which aids in reducing impulsivity and boosting focus and calm. Additionally, homeopathic therapies for ADHD don't have any negative side effects and won't worsen symptoms if you or your child try a different strategy.

You must take immediate action if your child is displaying violent behavior while experiencing signs of ADHD. It is a fact that children with ADHD who live in caring, nurturing environments occasionally lose control and hurt themselves or others. Consult a behavior therapist to prevent this from happening to your child, and consider beginning a homeopathic supplement program. You and your child will travel the road to health and pleasure more effectively.

HOW ADHD SYMPTOMS DIFFER IN WOMEN

Gender role demands complicate ADHD in women. The extensive societal demands placed on women, including taking care of oneself, the family, and the home, necessitate continual executive function coordination.

These expectations are not well suited for women with ADHD; however, they are frequently determined to achieve goals in their pursuit of social acceptance by disguising symptoms and issues. The dynamic interaction between societal expectations and executive dysfunction in ADHD is fueled by shame and self-blame. Clinicians must recognize how much women judge their values and self-esteem by their compliance with gender norms to understand women with ADHD.

The adjective "hyperactivity" is typically avoided when referring to adult Attention Deficit Hyperactivity Disorder because it is less common in adults than in children with ADHD.

Adults with ADHD who go years without managing, diagnosing, or treating the condition risk developing anxiety, depression, mood, or low self-esteem issues. Adults frequently believe that there is something fundamentally wrong with them as a person rather than realizing that there is a condition behind their troubles, even though they are aware that something is wrong. Poor memory, an inability to focus and concentrate on important tasks, fidgeting, and mind-wandering, among other symptoms, are the hallmark symptoms of ADHD in women. Since women tend to be less hyperactive than men, their symptoms may be milder and easier to ignore for some people. However, for others, these symptoms may be crippling and debilitating. Most are disjointed, tardy, inconsistent, dispersed, unorganized, and incompetent. Some claimed that labeling would continue even if women were already seeking medical attention and assistance. A woman with ADHD may appear boisterous, animated, overly exuberant, or even a thoughtful, imaginative person. In reality, seemingly simple activities at home, work, andsociety make her feel genuinely miserable. Because of specific bodily processes, such as hormonal shifts, women are also affected by ADHD differently. Additionally, these events make ADHD symptoms and signs worse, especially in older women just before menopause. As menopause draws near, many women with ADHD notice that their symptoms worsen, though they are frequently unsure what illness is to blame.

WHY ADHD IS UNDERDIAGNOSED IN WOMEN

Men and boys are more frequently diagnosed with ADHD than women and girls, even though it is not a male condition. Why? The presentation of ADHD in women is complicated by lingering preconceptions, referral bias, internalized symptoms, gender role expectations, comorbidities, and hormonal changes. Learn about typical symptoms of ADHD in women andthe challenges to a complete diagnosis and successful treatment in this chapter.

The underdiagnosis of ADHD in women dates back to early life. Girls with ADHD frequently work harder than men to disguise and make up for symptoms. Girls are frequently more eager to put in extra study time and ask for parental assistance to maintain their grades.

Girls are also more prone to be "people pleasers," going out of their way to fit in, even when they are aware of their "difference."

The first people to notice a child's symptoms of ADHD are frequently their teachers. However, because some teachers still believe that ADHD affects men more than women, they are more likely to suspect the disease in males than in girls. It doesn't matter if girls have the mixed, inattentive, or hyperactive form of the disorder—they might all be hyperactive and unable to sit still.

According to Patricia Quinn, M.D., a developmental pediatrician in Washington, D.C., who is a recognized authority on the gender characteristics of ADHD, "most people have a misconception that ADHD is a problem of hyperactive elementary school-aged boys. "Girls still go undetected even when they exhibit disruptive behaviors."

Different people experience ADHD in different ways. Boys with ADHD are diagnosed more frequently than girls for various complicated reasons. The most important ones are as follows:

Males have been the subject of most studies until recently, so more is known about how boys experience ADHD and how it affects their lives.

Researchers are focusing more on health disparities like this one at a time when awareness of income gaps and societal imbalances is growing. According to the CDC, boys are still diagnosed with ADHD 12.9 percent of the time compared to girls' 5.6 percent.

Is ADHD merely more prevalent in boys than in girls? Or does the culture around the disorder's research, diagnosis, and treatment largely favor boys? Researchers now understand that it is more complicated than that.

Many young girls with undiagnosed ADHD learn to identify with labels like "spacey," "far too talkative," and "disorganized" as they get older.

Even if their frustrated parents and teachers know that these young women are educated and talented, they may fall academically behind as teenagers. And many people still struggle with new roles and bigger responsibilities as adults.

Women with ADHD may be significantly impacted by the disparity in diagnostic rates and treatment access that results from those diagnoses. It impacts how they conduct their life, growstheir self-worth, and form connections.

Traditionally, most research on ADHD has been conducted on males. Males were thought to constitute about 80% of all people living with ADHD, and the DSM IV reported a 4:1 ratio between boys and girls with the disorder. Due to the lack of knowledge of ADHD in females, females with the disorder are frequently misdiagnosed and undertreated compared to males. So why are women ignored?

Girls struggle with quite different obstacles than boys and have several issues that differ from those in males with ADHD. Boys with ADHD engage in more disruptive activities at home and school and are more aggressive and belligerent. Despite tending to be physically hyperactive, girls are frequently timid and obedient and will engage in a quieter act of disorganization and inattention. Due to her lack of disruptive behavior, the girl draws little attention to herself or her problems, which delays, if not prevents, a diagnosis.

According to research, girls are not diagnosed until they are mid-30s-old women. This is because, until their children began to display the same symptoms and were eventually diagnosed, they were unaware that their lack of attention and frequently chaotic lives had a name.

Compared to the non-ADHD group, girls with ADHD were 16 times more likely to repeat a grade in school and over ten times more likely to be placed in special education.

In addition, they discovered that girls were less likely to be diagnosed with comorbid disorders like conduct disorder or oppositional defiant disorder compared to males. According to an additional study, women and girls with ADHD (especially if misdiagnosed) are more prone to experience sadness, anxiety, substance abuse, sexual promiscuity, and unintended pregnancies. The data mentioned above highlight how crucial it is to treat ADHD in girls as successfully and completely as it is treated in boys.

A persistent pattern of inattention, together with or without hyperactivity and impulsivity that interferes with daily functioning is the hallmark of ADHD, a neurological condition. Even if the incidence rates are getting closer between the sexes, the diagnosis rate for ADHD in Americans is 5.4% for males and 3.2% for women, a difference of about 69%.

Why? Stereotypes about female ADHD are untrue. Because of its specific symptom presentation, which is skewed toward inattentiveness, ADHD in women is still largely misunderstood, disregarded, and understudied.

Despite increased knowledge of ADHD in general, there is still much that science needs to understand and untangle regarding ADHD in women, particularly concerning how biology, neurology, and gender constructions affect the symptoms, progression, and course of therapy.

THE RIGHT DIAGNOSES FOR WOMEN WITH ADHD

Adult ADHD diagnoses have been rising for the last 10-15 years. This raises many questions for people, especially conspiracy theorists who wonder if this is another attempt for pharmaceutical companies to make more money with their medications.

However, the reality is that our awareness and understanding of ADHD as a condition has multiplied with ongoing research and our increased understanding of the brain.

For a long time now, ADHD has largely been thought only to affect school-aged children, and along with that misunderstanding, most people imagine a little boy who can't sit still in the classroom and is always getting into trouble.

This myth and inaccurate portrayal of ADHD keep people from getting the help they need, which can ultimately make a difference in their lives.

Dealing with adult ADHD symptoms can be difficult in and of itself. Many individuals with ADHD also deal with anxiety, depression, or obsessive-compulsive disorder. Additionally, they are more likely to smoke or take drugs. By receiving the appropriate therapy, people with ADHD can reduce these issues.

When taking medication for their ADHD, most adults see improvements, though others may still battle with bad habits and low self-esteem. Organization, creating useful routines, mending relationships, and enhancing social skills are the main goals of ADHD counseling. There is proof that cognitive-behavioral treatment is especially effective in treating everyday issues linked to ADHD.

Any person, regardless of age, is on the right route simply by knowing the diagnosis. Learning about ADHD, including its neurological causes, many manifestations, and typical difficulties, can be cathartic and therapeutic. Coaching and using a stimulant are beneficial when establishing new routines and habits. About 80% of the time, these drugs are effective, and the effects can feel completely transformative.

Of course, until doctors are aware of ADHD, especially as it affects adult women, none of this is probable or even achievable. A better understanding of ADHD in girls and women could have a profoundly positive impact on an infinite number of lives, and it might start a revolution in mental health, and I don't say that lightly.

The DSM, Fifth Edition, states three ADHD symptoms: primarily hyperactive, primarily inattentive, and combination type. Medical personnel frequently misinterpret and misdiagnose inattentive ADHD symptoms as mood disorders, anxiety, or another condition. Additionally, girls and women are more likely than boys and men to experience inattentive ADHD, contributing to the issue.

According to a reliable source, doctors treat girls with ADHD less frequently than boys by prescribing medication regularly. Sometimes it surprises me how prescription rates differ. According to the same study, stimulant and non-stimulant drugs help girls with most symptoms as much as they help boys, if not more.

Once more, it is conceivable to link these discrepancies to behavioral variations between boys and girls, which may lead to boys receiving therapy more frequently than girls.

Prescription rates are more comparable for adults. Even though the disparity is not as stark, women still take less medication than men.

There needs to be more investigation into how various people's bodies respond to medications for ADHD and how fluctuations in hormone levels affect how well the drugs work.

For instance, a 2007 study found that girls "wear off" stimulant drugs earlier in the day. By recognizing these variations, doctors could customize each woman's treatment.

WHY A PROMPT, CORRECT DIAGNOSIS IS IMPORTANT

Patients may face worse outcomes throughout a lifetime when a precise diagnosis and appropriate therapies are postponed. These consist of the following:
- less success in school and the workplace
- more despair and anxiety
- reduced self-esteem, greater marital conflict, physical symptoms such as headaches and stomach discomfort, and insomnia
- rising prices for healthcare

NON-MEDICAL TREATMENTS FOR ATTENTION DEFICIT

Making changes to the environment to support more fruitful social interactions is one of the non-drug treatments for ADHD. Among these modifications include adding more structure and promoting routines.

ADHD cannot be fully cured. However, several strategies can be used to lessen the effects of ADHD on those who have it.

1. MEDICINE

Doctors frequently administer stimulant or non-stimulant drugs to treat symptoms and enhance functioning when diagnosing ADHD in children and teenagers.

2. COUNSELING

Girls and women should discuss any additional hazards they may face as a result of having ADHD with therapists, according to a trusted source of medical specialists.

According to the experts, girls and women with ADHD are more likely to experience issues with substance use, behaviors that raise the risk of unfavorable outcomes, disordered eating, and self-harm.

3. COGNITIVE BEHAVIORAL THERAPY

Cognitive behavioral therapy (CBT) can assist people with ADHD in recognizing behavioral and thought patterns that exacerbate symptoms or impair executive function. People who receive treatment can improve their coping mechanisms and alter their feelings and behaviors.

This can eventually lessen how disruptive ADHD is to daily life.

4. INSTRUCTION IN SOCIAL SKILLS

A person's relationships and social interactions may suffer if they have ADHD. Women who haven't been diagnosed or got one later in life may have difficulty adjusting.

Because of this, teaching social skills to people with ADHD can facilitate their integration and foster relationships.

However, in a clinical environment, it isn't always successful.

Teaching persons with ADHD how to interact in real life may benefit their development. The review also makes the case thatinforming peers, and family members about ADHD's functioning and its effects on social integration may enable them to meet the demands of the individual better.

5. INFORMATION ON ADHD

Girls and women who are educated about ADHD may be able to seek stimulation that could negatively influence their coping mechanisms that, could cause more harm than good, feel guilty, and blame oneself

HOW IS WOMEN'S ADHD DIAGNOSED?

The poor diagnosis rate among women and girls is also due to outdated diagnostic criteria and presumptions. We've created the following symptom checklist for ladies to aid with that issue. Please respond to the following questions honestly and share the results with your mental health professional — the only one qualified to make an official diagnosis of ADHD symptoms — if you believe you or your daughter may have the disorder.

NOTE: This test is not meant to diagnose ADHD or to take the place of expert medical care.

You are more likely to have ADHD the more questions you correctly answer in the affirmative. Make sure to show your doctor your completed checklist.

ADHD IN ADULT WOMEN: SYMPTOMS CHECKLIST

- Do you have overwhelming feelings at gatherings, work, or the store? Do you find it difficult to block out noises and distractions that don't affect other people?
- Do things like time, money, paper, or "stuff" rule your life and prevent you from achieving your objectives?
- Do you frequently go into a trance during the day, feeling beaten? Do pleas for "one more thing" drive you to an emotional breaking point?
- Are you coping, hunting for things, catching up, or hiding most of the time? Do you stay away from others as a result?
- Have you stopped inviting guests over because you're embarrassed by the mess?
- Do you have issues with your checkbook balance?
- Do you frequently feel that life is out of control and fulfilling obligations is impossible?
- Do you feel like a couch potato or a tornado, perpetually at the extremes of a deregulated activity spectrum?
- Do you believe you are more creative than others but cannot arrange or implement your ideas?
- Do you get up every morning wanting to get organized yet feel defeated every night?
- Have you seen people of your age and intelligence walk past you?
- Do you doubt your ability to reach your potential and achieve your objectives?
- Have you ever been accused of being ungrateful because you don't send people birthday cards or thank you notes?
- Do you know how other people manage to have constant, routine lives?

- Are they calling you "spacey" or "a slob"? Are you trying to appear normal? Do you ever feel like an impostor?
- Is all your time and effort going toward dealing, maintaining organization, and keeping it together, leaving you with little spare time for leisure or fun?

Once a patient knows her condition, she can capitalize on the skills and abilities linked to ADHD. Finding their gifts requires receiving an ADHD diagnosis, not managing their problem. In women, ADHD manifests differently.

Here are the How and Why.

Both sexes are equally affected by ADHD, but due to outmoded stereotypes, many women go untreated and experience hopelessness, stupidity, or depression. In girls or women, ADHD frequently presents differently. Unfortunately, many professionals could still have trouble correctly diagnosing their ADHD, which can impede receiving good treatment.

There isn't much in which American women haven't made significant progress in recent years, from work possibilities to personal finances to marriage relationships. But when it comes to acquiring an ADHD diagnosis and receiving treatment, women still have a long way to go.

THE DIAGNOSIS SHOULD BE MADE BY WHO?

In Silver Spring, Maryland, clinical psychologist Kathleen Nadeau, Ph.D., oversees a private practice that identifies and manages learning problems and ADHD. She claims that after years of trying to juggle the demands of work, a home, and raising children, many women begin to suspect that they have ADHD.

After reading about ADHD in the media, some women start to question the source of their issues. After learning that their child has ADHD, other moms wonder if they, too, do.

In any event, many of the women who seek Nadeau's help do so only after experiencing frustration for months or years while their concerns went unresolved by medical professionals.

Depression is frequently diagnosed in women before they are given an ADHD diagnosis, according to Nadeau. "So many women have visited my office and said, "I've been in therapy for years; I have anxiety and depression diagnoses, yet I still have problems. It's frustrating, yet the illness is so easily curable, and there's no justification for that.

Because the criteria used by doctors to diagnose ADHD are antiquated, many women, according to Nadeau, go without receiving a diagnosis. For instance, the criteria state that ADHD should only be considered a possible diagnosis if the patient has had substantial symptoms since a young age. However, many girls with ADHD "slip under the radar" in the early stages of the illness, as doctors are beginning to learn.

ADHD IN WOMEN: DIAGNOSTIC ISSUES AND DIFFICULTIES

Clinicians use rating scales, interviews, and other techniques to diagnose ADHD in addition to the DSM-5 recommendations. According to research, these diagnostic criteria consistently result in under-identification and under-diagnosis of ADHD in girls and women compared to boys and men. These factors are among the causes of this difference.

1. The Presentation Of Inattentive Symptoms In Women With Adhd

Many women and girls with ADHD, who are not overtly disruptive to others, exhibit modest symptom presentation with a higher likelihood of inattentiveness. However, the hyperactive, disruptive ADHD presentations that are more prevalent in males and boys are most familiar to many therapists. According to studies, compared to other ADHD presentations, hyperactivity, impulsivity, and other externalizing symptoms (such as conduct difficulties) are strong predictors of diagnosis. Camouflaging signs include: According to research, women are highly driven to cover up and make up for their ADHD symptoms. The apparent symptoms are frequently anxiety- or mood-related, which can result in misdiagnosis.

2. The Gender Bias In Adhd In Women

Although it is rarely deliberate, gender bias is sneaky and persistent, affecting how doctors view and categorize women.

Referrals: Few girls and teenagers with inattentive, non-disruptive symptoms are sought for diagnosis or consultation since they rarely cause concern.

Rating scales for ADHD continue to favor signs of masculine behavior. Many assessments are not normed for women's values, and internalized symptoms and limitations are frequently ignored.

3. Adhd In Women: The Role Of Hormones

All women's physical, social, and emotional health depends on ovarian hormones, which interact with every body system. Because estrogen protects the brain by increasing neurotransmitter activity, which also affects executive function, attention, motivation, verbal memory, sleep, and concentration, the brain is a target organ for estrogen.

Throughout the month and throughout a person's life, estrogen levels change, affecting how symptoms of ADHD manifest in women. The common perception of ADHD is that its symptoms are consistent over time; however, this is not the case for women.

The symptoms of ADHD change with hormonal changes. The symptoms of ADHD worsen when estrogen levels fall, and estrogen levels decline just before the start of menstruation. The low estrogen and high progesterone ratio greatly aggravate the symptoms.

Additionally, it implies that symptoms may change daily. Even more sensitive to these micro-fluctuations may be some women.

During puberty, around the time that girls' symptoms of ADHD start to stand out more, estrogen comes into play. These hormonal changes frequently manifest as worry and emotional turbulence. Still, they may also be particularly intense during this period, resulting in a false diagnosis of anxiety or a mood illness and inadequate or incorrect treatment.

CONSIDERATIONS FOR TREATMENT OF ADHD IN WOMEN

Therapy, medication, lifestyle modifications, and accommodations can all be used to manage ADHD. The following therapies should be taken into consideration for women with ADHD:

A doctor who has experience treating girls and women with ADHD. The most crucial and challenging task is probably to find this expert. Make sure to inquire about their experience managing women's ADHD.

Family psychoeducation: Your family and friends must comprehend ADHD as well.

Reframing: Therapists can assist you in validating your experience, exploring the influence of societal norms on your perspective, and learning self-advocacy skills.

Medication: It's crucial to locate a doctor knowledgeable about how hormones affect ADHD and how they interact with prescription drugs. For instance, stimulants could be less effective later in the menstrual cycle. Hormone replacement therapy significantly reduces ADHD symptoms in postmenopausal women by increasing progesterone and estrogen levels in the body. Clinicians must comprehend how stimulants interact with SSRIs and affect symptoms generally because SSRIs are frequently recommended for anxiety and mood disorders.

Rearranging your environment to fit your needs better: Therapists and other specialists can assist you in learning how to rearrange your environment.

And ideas to fit your lifestyle.

Coaching and support groups can both help you achieve your goals. Support groups can assist in normalizing the experience of having ADHD and lessen feelings of loneliness, worry, and distress.

WHY THE SUDDEN INCREASE IN ADULT ADHD?

There is still more we don't know or understand about ADHD, and it is one of those conditions that continue to surprise and cause controversy at almost every corner. What once was believed only to affect little boys is known to be present equally among boys and girls. We also used to believe that children outgrew their symptoms of ADHD and that the condition disappeared with age.

However, through further investigation, study, awareness, and closer examination of the brain, we understand that ADHD does not simply go away or disappear in adulthood.

ADHD is a lifespan condition that changes as an individual age or faces new challenges. What we once thought was the disappearance of symptoms turned out to be a lessening of hyperactivity with maturity.

We also discovered adults who learned to manage their symptoms and difficulties by finding the right career or developing the right support.

BUT WHAT ABOUT THOSE WHO STILL STRUGGLE?

Even though there is a part of the population who has successfully learned to manage their struggles, there are still many adults who are stuck believing they are lazy, crazy, or even stupid. But that's not the case.

Unfortunately, many people are faced with difficulties simply because they aren't aware of the reality and impact that ADHD has on an individual.

Now I'm not particularly big on labels, research, and focusing on a diagnosis. However, I firmly believe that we understand what impacts us so everyone can get the support, resources, help, and skills needed to succeed at work, in relationships, andin life.

Some people benefit from being diagnosed with ADHD or adult ADHD;others do not. What's important here is that you know what might be causing difficulties for you or a loved one.

THE GOOD SIDE OF ADHD IN WOMEN

When you went your child or children to the doctor to find out why they were having trouble paying attention, were you astonished to realize that you had ADHD? You probably also learned that there is a 25 to 35% chance that your child would get ADHD if you do. You're not to a fault! You are not to blame. It's just basic biology over which you have no influence, and if you approach it with a pessimistic mindset, it can make you depressed.

On the other hand, you might have felt relieved to finally have an explanation for emotions you've been experiencing since childhood but haven't been able to name them. Now is not the time to say anything negative! Concentrate on your assets and liabilities, and you'll likely let go of your negative emotions. Success with ADHD results from the positive activity for you and your ADHD-affected child.

When you have a family and are married, you can discover that your ADHD tendencies make life hard. In American households, the woman has typically been in charge of maintaining order, but this is changing. Guilt may also play a role when you're down and out and can't quite live up to society's expectations. When you work outside the home, the situation is made worse.

You require assistance with ADHD-friendly methods.

There are schedules at work that work well with your ADHD if you perform well at work but struggle to make things work at home. But typically, our homes don't have the same layouts, and everything happens as it does. Making routines at home, however, can be a terrific method to reduce your stress levels, especially if you work outside the home and have limited free time to manage the demands of family life.

You don't have to do all the household duties. Some of the household duties should be handled by your partner, and if you have children, you might be able to assign some of them to them, depending on their ages. They should be capable of performing simple tasks, such as setting the table, around the age of five.

As youngsters age, assign them more difficult tasks like laundry sorting. They can and ought to assist you and take over some of the tasks that are falling through the gaps but that you are supposed to have completed.

Additionally, please do not consider it to be dumping your obligations on your kids. Even if that is a benefit, the goal should instill a sense of responsibility in them. They will learn the value of money if you give them an allowance in exchange for their work. What an amazing thing!

Next, select what duties you are solely responsible for performing and add them to your schedule. For instance, clean up the carpets on Monday. Maybe the grocery shop on Tuesday could be wash day on Wednesday. Get a planner you can always refer to, write everything down, or use an electronic version that will schedule repetitive activities. But suddenly, they don't appear as intimidating when you put everything in writing. Plus, everything will be there before you, so you won't have to worry about not remembering to do something. It may also be beneficial to wake up and fall asleep at roughly the same time each day. Eat your main meals simultaneously every day, engage in activities with your children simultaneously each day, etc. While not everything needs to be planned out, you'll feel safer if you have a general notion of what happens during the day. Additionally, if you have a job that requires you to commute, consider scheduling "nights" like "pizza night," "fun night," and "learning night," or something similar. Knowing what to do when you're too exhausted to think clearly will be helpful.

Pay close attention if you experience ADHD-related rage episodes. Be careful not to lash out at your kids when things get too busy. Things can become chaotic while preparing a meal as the kids get into trouble, the TV is on, and the cat is trying to trip you at every turn. Please don't allow it to drive you crazy and make you want to scream! You are aware that there are some things we cannot control, and when we are attempting to focus but are unable to, distractions make us irritable. So, ask someone else to referee in the family room when you're working on something complicated, like cooking. Ask your partner or another person available to babysit the children in another room while you focus on what has to be done without interruption. Or avoid cooking! When you consider the time required to go out and buy the food, cook the dinner, etc., catering isn't as pricey as you might assume. Maybe it wouldn't be such a horrible idea to have someone else provide your meals.

But why not make them while the kids are at school and store the food in the refrigerator or freezer until right before supper if you love to cook, can't afford to go out frequently, or have meals brought in? Or, if you're a single parent, how about getting a nanny to watch the kids while you work on something as challenging as cooking a delicious meal? Any situation can have a budget-friendly system that is ADHD-friendly. But things still happen no matter how hard you try to plan. Go into another room for a while when you feel like you might burst to give yourself some space to calm down and regain your composure. Give yourself time to regain perspective on the situation. Emotional outbursts are not helpful to you or others or a solution to your issues, and they'll only worsen your guilt.

In addition to substance usage, ADHD women are more likely to hide their issues from others, including their closest confidants. Smoking, drinking, and using drugs are all examples of self-medication. All of this won't do anything to assist your ADHD; all you want is to feel better. Don't wait to get expert assistance if you suspect you're becoming dependent on anything. Numerous solutions are available to you that won't harm you or your loved ones. All you need to do is understand what they are and how to use them.Initially, give up blaming yourself. You didn't ask for ADHD, but in some ways, it's a big plus. You are, without a doubt, quite intelligent, and you have an extraordinary aptitude for concentration and think faster and more creatively than others. Recognize that these qualities make you unique, and focus on opportunities rather than challenges. There is no reason to feel depressed about attention deficit. It makes you unique, but it could negatively affect your life if you don't focus on understanding your advantages and disadvantages. Finding out you have ADHD may provide you access to new opportunities. Utilize your advantages and come up with ADHD-friendly solutions to your weaknesses. It's okay if you require expert assistance to complete this. What you need, ask for. That is the first step toward improving one's mental state.

RAISING ADHD AWARENESS EVERY DAY

Since 2004, the United States Congress has devoted one September day to National ADHD Awareness Day. ADHD is becoming a major health problem in the United States, and National ADHD Day hopes to encourage everyone to learn more about this disorder, support ADHD services, and find ways to seek treatment and help.

However, you don't need to wait for September to garner support and awareness for ADHD, especially if this disorder afflicts someone you love. Here are some ways you can raise ADHD awareness no matter what day of the year it is.

EDUCATE YOURSELF

The first step to raising awareness for ADHD is to arm yourself with information. Read all you can about ADHD, its causes, and available treatments. Borrow books from the library and read voraciously.

Look into the pros and cons of using stimulants as a primary treatment, and open your mind to the many new ways to treat ADHD without drugs. Scientific journals are a great source of reliable studies on ADHD, while websites like sciencedaily.com and webmd.com provide easy-to-read news on treatments and ongoing research.

JOIN A PARENT-TEACHER ORGANIZATION

If you have a child with ADHD, their behavior may be widely misunderstood by teachers and classmates. Or perhaps your child isn't receiving the special education services they need. Joining a parent-teacher organization is a great way to inform educators about ADHD, its symptoms, and the myths surrounding this disorder.

Raising awareness about ADHD at school can also help teachers identify the disorder among students and suggest an evaluation to their parents. If obtaining special services for your child is your goal, do your homework - read up on special education laws, your child's rights, and the ways you can protect these rights. Find ways to negotiate with the school so your child can get the appropriate special education services.

ESTABLISH A SUPPORT GROUP

Anyone who has studied or dealt with ADHD for years is in a great position to help others know more about the disorder. You can start a support group for parents, friends, and family members of someone with the disorder. Point them toward resources that can broaden their understanding of ADHD and help them find ways to cope with the difficulties of having a loved one with ADHD.

CORRECT ADHD DOUBTERS AS THEY COME

ADHD is not the most pleasant conversation topic at social gatherings, but there is no better time to correct misconceptions about the disorder than encountering a doubter. The research you have done should help you respond to questions and statements from skeptics, such as:

- Is ADHD even a real disorder?
- Won't children outgrow ADHD?
- ADHD is just an excuse for lazy behavior or poor parenting.
- ADHD is just for children.
- Your child needs more discipline.

HOW TO MANAGE EMOTIONS IN A WOMAN WITH ADHD

People with ADHD have a lot going for them. They possess exceptional intelligence, creativity, and intuition. However, ADHD also makes you sensitive and may prevent you from expressing your emotions. It doesn't matter if you're a guy or a woman; some feelings aren't acceptable in society.

Most people spend a significant portion of each day concealing their genuine emotions. However, did you realize that doing this frequently can harm you?

The pancreas, thyroid, parathyroid, thymus, pituitary, adrenal, pineal, and gonad glands, which are your sexual organs, are among the endocrine system's glands. Each of these glands has unique nutritional needs and reacts differently. This system interacts to respond when we experience emotions. No matter how hard we try, the process cannot be stopped. We can upset the balance by suppressing and denying our feelings; if we do so frequently, we risk being ill.

But most of the time, society makes it difficult to express our feelings fully. It's extremely harder if you have ADHD and sense that you're slipping out of control. People with ADHD find it extremely unpleasant, so we reject it when emotion comes on suddenly.

That's not good, though. There must be a way to express emotions. Instead of suppressing any unpleasant feelings you may be experiencing, find a quiet area where you can be alone and just let the negativity out.

Anger is one emotion connected to ADHD, and it typically stems from irritation and fear. Being in unfamiliar circumstances can be stressful since you never know what will occur next. You may also become frustrated if you know that you have a deadline but keep getting sidetracked and unable to complete the task. You feel frustrated, and that feeling can occasionally go out of control. When that occurs, remember that regardless of whether a person has ADD, everyone feels emotions. The problem is in how you respond to those emotions.

Screaming into a pillow in a quiet spot is one method to get your rage out. Alternatively, if you must break something because you are so angry, choose something little, like a pencil. The snap frequently aids in calming your irrational emotions.

Remember that emotions don't go away when you become an adult, especially if you have a sensitive nature. When emotions are strong, find a technique to let them out that won't harm you or anybody else. You risk making yourself quite ill if you don't, which is not wise. Grab a pillow instead, and kick it around the room. Even though the pillow won't feel great, you'll be completely fine.

RIGHT NUTRITION FOR A WOMAN WITH ADHD

Some experts say ADHD symptoms may be lessened by foods that give great brain fuel. Nuts, pork, beans, and eggs are high-protein diets that may enhance concentration. Substituting complex carbohydrates, such as whole-grain pasta or brown rice, for simple carbohydrates can reduce the occurrence of mood swings and maintain energy levels.

DOES SUGAR MAKE ADHD WORSE?

There is a common belief that sugar makes people hyperactive; however, there is no proof that sweets cause ADHD or exacerbate its symptoms. According to research on kids, switching to a sugar substitute like aspartame does not lessen ADHD symptoms.

Mild food allergies can bring on adult ADHD without the person's awareness of the sensitivity. Since the symptoms of these minor food allergies are common to many different causes, they sometimes go unnoticed for a long period. One of the signs of ADHD is difficulty focusing. The quickest technique to ascertain if you have one of these mild food allergies is to perform a diet test where you gradually cut out and add various foods to your diet while keeping track of how you feel and how well you can concentrate.

AN ADULT ADHD DIET AUDIT PROCEDURE

Start by compiling a list of all the food categories you typically eat and want to test. Here is a list of frequent food allergies:

- Sugar, dairy products, fish, seafood, beef (fatty meats), grains, corn, wheat, apples, grapes, bananas, MSG, yeast, and chocolate.
- Artificial Preservatives & Artificial Colors
- Nut, butter, citrus, and nuts

Eliminate Each Food One at a Time and Keep Track - Start with the first food and cut it out of your diet for at least three days. Keep a daily journal detailing your feelings and your level of concentration. Keep track of any non-food factors in your journal that can influence how you think or feel so that you can look for trends. Women may discover that their menstrual cycle also impacts their ADD; they may want to note this since it can skew the findings of your meal test.

After a few days, bring that food back into your diet. Then, keep track of your progress. Repeat the technique with the following item on the list after waiting a day to see how adding that food type has affected you. Continue doing this until the list is finished. If you kept solid daily records, you should be able to determine which foods had a favorable impact on your well-being when you eliminated them from your diet and a negative impact when you reintroduced them.

View Your Results - It's crucial that you only test one food type at a time and that you eat regularly, aside from the item being tested when performing this test. By doing this, you can get more precise findings and determine which meals aren't compatible with your body. If you discover that a certain meal has a bad effect on you, work on removing it from your diet. If you are genuinely worried, you might wish to discuss the results of this test with your doctor.

AN EFFECTIVE METHOD FOR COPING WITH ADHD

Effect on Everyday Life Research has found that women with ADHD frequently have extremely low self-esteem. Compared to adult men with ADHD, they also appear to have higher emotional and psychological suffering.

Some women can conceal their symptoms, depending on the degree of their illness, to avoid embarrassment and rejection. Others who have ADHD could feel as though their lives are in complete disarray. Since women are often in charge of caring for the home and children, this may have an impact on the entire family, according to data.

Ineffective coping mechanisms might negatively impact your daily life and amplify your difficulties. For instance, you could find it challenging to manage the obligations of your job, prepare regular meals for your family, or keep up with other housework. Having a constant sense of attempting to catch up might cause chronic stress and tiredness.

If any of these symptoms ring a bell, seek the advice of a medical professional or a therapist.

THERAPY ALTERNATIVES

In contrast to children, medication is the first line of treatment for adults with ADHD. Although medication cannot treat ADHD, it may reduce symptoms and simplify daily life.

Psychostimulants are the term for ADHD drugs. They directly impact the brain chemicals that regulate your attention and behavioral problems. The two most widely used stimulants are:

Amphetamines containing methylphenidate (Concerta, Daytrana, Focalin, Focalin XR, and Metadate) (Adderall and Vyvanse)

Until they find the best medication for you, doctors may prescribe you various low-dose medications to try for 3–7 days. They will also consider your other medical conditions when deciding which meds are best for you. Inform your doctor of all other health issues you may have, including prescription and over-the-counter medications, herbal remedies, and dietary supplements you may be using.

In addition to medication, your doctor may also recommend a combination of therapies that teaches you coping mechanisms, self-esteem, and life management skills, such as psychotherapy, stress management, and another ADHD-focused coaching. Whether you require them will depend on your unique symptoms and circumstances.

Parent training and other therapy may be helpful for mothers with ADHD, and this can assist you in managing your duties to your children more effectively. A support group is another option for meeting others who can connect to what you're going through, and groups can help you develop the social skills you need for everyday living.

You can speak with a career counselor who is aware of ADHD if you have trouble keeping up with the demands of your employment. They could encourage you to build on your strengths to manage your work performance effectively.

ADDITIONAL RESEARCH IS REQUIRED

Scientists believe they need more research on gender differences in the condition as more adult women seek therapy and diagnosis for ADHD.

For instance, some professionals think that female hormones may influence young girls' and women's ADHD symptoms, and females may require different care than boys or men. Additionally, many girls are brought up to behave differently from boys, and this can cause people to demonstrate their ADHD symptoms in different ways.

In the end, specialists claim that additional research can aid in the early detection, diagnosis, and treatment of ADHD symptoms in young girls and women. That improved long-term management of the illness depends on early intervention.

HOW TO TREAT ADHD IN WOMEN

When it comes to managing ADHD, women might not be as helpless. Greater efficiency, coordination, and self-control can be developed with the help of medicine and treatment, which can positively impact women's overall well-being.

Research suggests that there is a substantial hereditary predisposition to ADHD. Women with ADHD frequently have a family history of the condition. Getting the correct medical personnel to diagnose the condition might help to manage it.

Treatment options include prescription medications, psychological therapies, and natural or complementary methods of symptom management. The most common treatment doctors recommend for adults with ADHD is the prescription drug Adderall or another stimulant substance like Ritalin or Concerta.

Some women only need medicine to treat their adult ADHD symptoms, but a rigid, self-imposed set of behavior modifications may be the best course for others. Without medication, ADHD symptoms can be reduced by implementing these and other beneficial behavioral adjustments. Similar behavioral modification approaches are successfully used by many therapists who treat women with ADHD.

The vast majority of those who employ such tactics claim improvement. A therapist can also assist an ADHD patient in coping with concerns with family members, guilt, shame, or a sense of failure that may come with a history of battling with the condition. In addition, experts suggest that many women with ADHD may benefit from joining a support group to help regulate problem behaviors and increase productivity. This is in addition to working with a therapist.

DRUGS FOR ADHD AND THEIR SIDE EFFECTS

Your treatment plan for ADHD must include medication. To treat the disorder's symptoms, doctors have access to various medications.

Together, you and your doctor will decide which medication is best for you, as well as the proper dose (amount) and schedule (how often or when you need to take it). Finding the ideal combination could take some time.

Not all ADHD symptoms respond to medication, and not everyone is affected similarly. The best treatments frequently combine medication, therapy, behavior modifications, and skill development, referred to as multimodal therapy.

The ones that are used most frequently to treat ADHD are:

STIMULANTS.
This class of medications has been used for many years to treat ADHD. You may be able to concentrate and block out distractions with these medications. 70% to 80% of persons report success with stimulant medications to treat moderate and severe ADHD. They might be useful for kids, teens, and adults who struggle at school, work, or home. Some stimulants can be used by kids older than three, and others are okayed for kids older than six.

NON-STIMULANTS.
Non-stimulants could be useful when stimulants are ineffective or have undesirable side effects. These drugs can help with symptoms including focus and impulse control.

ANTIDEPRESSANTS.
Bipolar illness, anxiety, and sadness are also frequently present in people with ADHD. Along with a stimulant for ADHD, they may also take an antidepressant to manage other diseases or mental health difficulties.

SHORT-ACTING STIMULANTS: TYPES AND EFFECTS
Short-acting stimulants can cause tics, weight loss, sleep issues, irritability, and loss of appetite. It would help if you regularly took them.
Concerning the possibility of drug misuse with amphetamine stimulants, the FDA has issued a warning. According to FDA safety experts, all amphetamine and methylphenidate stimulants used to treat ADHD raise the risk of heart and psychiatric problems.

TYPES OF NON-STIMULANT ADHD DRUGS AND ADVERSE REACTIONS
It typically takes some time for non-stimulant drugs to start working. You might not feel the full results for a few weeks, and they might not function as well as stimulants. Some non-stimulant drugs may make youth more likely to have suicidal thoughts and die by suicide. The FDA advises monitoring for suicidal thoughts in anyone using atomoxetine (Strattera), especially in the first few weeks. These medications frequently cause fatigue, stomach trouble, dry mouth,

and nausea as adverse effects. Frequently, when you stop taking them, your blood pressure increases.

TYPES OF ANTIDEPRESSANT ADHD DRUGS AND ADVERSE REACTIONS

Off-label use of these drugs is permitted to treat ADHD symptoms, implying that even if the FDA has not approved them for ADHD, doctors can still prescribe them. Sleep issues, motion sickness, constipation, dry mouth, sweating, and changes in sex drive are common side effects. Antidepressants have been linked to an increased risk of suicide in adults ages 18 to 24, particularly in the first one or two months, according to another FDA warning.

ASSOCIATED ADHD DRUGS AND SAFETY

In general, experts believe that these medications are secure when properly managed by a professional. Serious issues are uncommon. Describe to your doctor the advantages and disadvantages of these medications.

ADHD AND OTHER CONDITIONS ARE TREATED

A second mental health issue, such as anxiety, depression, personality disorders, or substance use disorders, affects up to 80% of people with ADHD. Both these problems and how they are treated can impact ADHD. For instance, some stimulant drugs may exacerbate anxiety symptoms. However, your doctor can frequently safely combine medicines for ADHD and depression. Your entire mental health will determine your treatment plan.

HOW TO USE EXERCISE IN TREATING ADHD IN WOMEN

Exercise can enhance your mood, lower your risk of heart disease, give you more energy, boost your self-esteem, help you sleep better, improve your memory, and slow the aging process. Yet most of us still come up with several justifications for not working out.
We could ramble on for hours about the advantages of regular exercise.
Although most know that exercise improves our mood, we don't all understand why. We assume that it's because we're releasing stress, relaxing tight muscles, or increasing endorphins, and we leave it at that. However, the true reason we feel so wonderful after exercising is that it improves brain function. In my opinion, this effect of exercise is far more significant and fascinating than what it does for the body. The heart and lungs are strengthened, and muscles develop as a side effect. I remind my patients that exercise aims to strengthen and improve the brain.
According to the most recent study, exercise can maintain the brain healthy into old age and may prevent Alzheimer's disease and other aging-related mental illnesses. The University of California at Irvine's Carl Cotman, Ph.D., discovered a connection between physical activity and mental capacity. In a study published in Nature, Cotman summarised that exercise could regulate the molecules necessary for the brain's health. Rodents were used in Cotman's study because, according to him, "the benefits of exercise are essentially equivalent in people and rats." Cotman saw "couch" rats and treadmill-running rats in his study. Brain-derived neurotrophic factor (BDNF), the brain's most extensively distributed growth factor and one thought to deteriorate with the development of Alzheimer's disease, was significantly more prevalent in the rats that exercised.
Exercise encourages the growth of new neurons in the brain and enhances the connections between existing neurons. Memory and learning-related brain regions are those that are stimulated by exercise. In Cotman's words:
I believe that's a fascinating takeaway message because it shows that if you're in good shape, you may be able to learn and perform more efficiently. One of the notable benefits of exercise, which is occasionally underappreciated in research, is an enhancement in the learning rate.

A 2007 German study found that the learning rate was closely connected with levels of BDNF in the brain and that people learn vocabulary items 20% faster after exercise than before exercise.

Exercise is a fantastic approach to boosting your emotions and mood. Your body feels calmer and more relaxed after exercise. Learn some causes and the most effective exercises for mood enhancement and emotional balance.

When exercising, your brain releases dopamine, endorphins, adrenaline, and serotonin. Together, these substances help you feel happy. Additionally, you might feel accomplished after working out, and your muscles will relax more deeply, reducing tension and strain. Dr. Jeremy Sibold, professor of rehabilitation and movement science at the University of Vermont, Burlington, the study's primary researcher, said that moderate-intensity aerobic exercise immediately improves mood, and those gains can persist for up to 12 hours.

EXERCISE INCREASES ENERGY AND FIGHTS FATIGUE.

Are you fatigued? If you want to increase your energy and battle exhaustion, a walk might be preferable to a nap.

According to recent studies, regular exercise can boost energy levels even in those with debilitating chronic illnesses like cancer and heart disease.

Although it may seem paradoxical, researchers claim that regularly exercising can help you feel more energetic in the long run.

The last thing individuals want to do when they are tired is exercise, according to researcher Patrick O'Connor, Ph.D., in a news release. But being a little bit more active will assist if you're physically exhausted and inactive, according to O'Connor, co-director of the University of Georgia's exercise psychology lab in Athens, Georgia. According to researcher Tim Puetz, Ph.D., also of UGA, "We live in a society where individuals are continually looking for the next sports drink, energy snack, or a cup of coffee that will give them the extra edge to get through the day." But it's possible that putting on your sneakers, going outside, and exercising every morning can give people the energy they need.

The researchers examined data from more than 6,800 participants in 70 studies on exercise and exhaustion for this study, which was published in Psychological Bulletin.

Compared to groups that did not exercise, sedentary adults who completed a regular exercise program experienced less fatigue, according to more than 90% of the trials, according to O'Connor. It has a fairly reliable impact.

The findings demonstrate that regular exercise boosts energy and lessens weariness.

The average effect outweighed the benefits of using stimulant drugs, including those for narcolepsy and attention deficit hyperactivity disorder (ADHD).

Nearly every group investigated, including healthy adults, cancer patients, and people with chronic diseases like diabetes and heart disease, benefited from exercise, according to researchers.

Jackson, my former patient, is a slim 21-year-old with an untucked shirt and jeans who chats intelligently about his future goals. He is a normal American college student, if not a little smarter. Not so much where he is now as how far he has come and how he did it with an alternative ADHD treatment stand out about him.

Jack has attention deficit hyperactivity disorder (ADHD or ADD) and runs almost daily, covering three to six miles, depending on whether he also does resistance training that day. It's not like I feel guilty if I don't do it, he claims. "I want to do something because I feel like I missed it during the day. I discovered that I don't have any trouble focusing on anything while I'm exercising, so for that reason."

When Jackson's third-grade teacher noticed his obnoxious conduct and inability to complete classwork, she immediately diagnosed him with ADHD. He started using Ritalin and continued to use a stimulant throughout his years in school.

He had too much work to go through as a day student at a prestigious private academy. I once prescribed him clonazepam, a long-acting anxiety medication, Paxil, and Adderall.

Despite having familial ties, Jackson barely passed with a 1.8 GPA—far too low to enroll in the college he had intended to attend. He was nonetheless admitted to a modest junior college, which was good. After graduating from college, he was at the top of the world and knew where he would live the following fall. He felt so fantastic that summer that he decided to stop taking his medicine completely. (It goes without saying that I wasn't informed then.) He notes, "I found that many little things that upset me went away.

The summer's true turning point occurred while he was traveling with his girlfriend to Spain. He was motivated to address his Buddha belly after seeing so many "Spanish dudes" while walking around the beach shirtless. He recalls, "I just started to run." "And I began to feel fantastic."

I find Jackson's experience interesting partly because he started working out to improve his body image but continued because of the therapeutic benefits. Initially, the running didn't do much for his physique (thanks to the pizza and beer), but he persisted since it improved his concentration. With a 3.9 GPA in his first semester at the junior college, he was admitted as a transfer student to the college he had initially intended to attend after a year.

Jackson is well aware of his mental state. His focus deteriorates if he abandons his exercise routine, and knowing how it makes him feel keeps him going because he is aware of it. When he began working out, he recalls, "I suddenly was able to focus on things that were essential to me." "The link between exercise and attention has never been in doubt. Things in my life started to change after I committed to exercising and made this significant life shift.

Not every person with ADHD will benefit as greatly from exercise as Jackson did. And I never would have advised him to stop taking his medication suddenly, especially the antidepressant. His experience raises the question of whether exercise can take the place of Ritalin, Adderall, or Wellbutrin, and I would suggest that the answer is generally no. At least not in the way exercise can replace Zoloft in treating mood disorders, as demonstrated by James Blumenthal, Ph.D., and his associates at Duke University.

Jackson's reasoning for stopping his medication is educational in several ways. He was smart enough to succeed, but I believe he felt out of control because he was powerless to make it happen. Demoralization can result from ongoing frustration, which in Jackson's case, fueled his mental condition. He experienced a sense of dependency after taking medication, which exacerbated his feelings. On the other hand, establishing a jogging habit gave him a sense of control over his inner self, including his mood, anxiety, and focus. He felt like he had control over his destiny for the first time. Running served as his treatment.

ACTIVATE THE MIND
According to general science, exercise reduces ADHD by raising neurotransmitters norepinephrine and dopamine levels, which are crucial for controlling the attention system. We can increase the baseline levels of dopamine and norepinephrine with regular exercise by promoting the development of new receptors in specific brain regions.

In the arousal area of the brain stem, exercise also helps maintain norepinephrine balance. According to Amelia Russo-Neustadt, M.D., Ph.D., a neuroscientist and psychiatrist at California State University, "Chronic exercise enhances the tone of the locus coeruleus." We are less likely to be startled or respond inappropriately to any given scenario and less agitated.

Similar to this, I consider exercise to be the basal ganglia's transmission fluid, which facilitates the seamless shifting of the attention system. The brain scans of children with ADHD reveal abnormalities in this region, which is the major binding site for stimulants.

Through motor-function tests, which offer proximate indicators of dopamine activity, one team of researchers, led by Rodney Dishman, Ph.D. of the University of Georgia, investigated the effects of exercise in ADHD children. Dishman was shocked by the results since boys and girls had different answers. Boys who engaged in vigorous exercise improved certain motor reflex inhibition behaviors, such as sticking out their tongues and maintaining a straight face.

The lack of improvement in girls may be due to their lower prevalence of hyperactivity. Another measure of dopamine synapses' sensitivity showed improvements in both boys and girls. However, males performed better after maximal (vigorous) activity and girls after submaximal (moderate) exercise.

There are positive impacts of exercise on many parts of the brain. Children with ADHD often have a hyperactive cerebellum, which can cause fidgetiness. Recent research has revealed that ADHD drugs that increase dopamine and norepinephrine can restore balance in this area. The more challenging the exercise, the better it is for raising norepinephrine levels. Scientists have studied the neurochemical changes in rats' brains following periods of acrobatic training, which is the closest thing to judo for rats (at least for now). Rats who performed difficult motor skills saw a more substantial increase in brain-derived neurotrophic factor (BDNF) levels than their treadmill-running counterparts, which may indicate cerebellar expansion.

For adults and children with ADHD, any form of martial arts, ballet, ice skating, gymnastics, rock climbing, mountain biking, whitewater paddling, and-sorry to break it to you, Mom-skateboarding is particularly beneficial. Exactly why? A wide range of brain regions that regulate balance, timing, sequencing, evaluating consequences, switching, error correction, fine motor adjustments, inhibition, and, of course, intense attention and concentration are activated by the precise movement inherent in these forms of sports.

The fight-or-flight response is activated when participating in these activities because, in the extreme, doing so involves surviving (e.g., evading a karate chop, drowning in a whirling pool of whitewater, or breaking your neck on the balance beam). When the mind is on high alert, there is plenty of motivation to pick up the abilities required for these pursuits. The brain operates on a "do or die" basis. Of course, the majority of the time we spend engaging in these activities will be spent in the aerobic range, which improves our cognitive function and facilitates learning new techniques.

Because it helps to control the amygdala, exercise is also beneficial for the limbic system. The amygdala tempers the hair-trigger hypersensitivity that many individuals with ADHD experience and balances out the response to new stimuli, preventing us from losing control and yelling at another driver in a fit of road rage, for instance. The prefrontal cortex's functionality is crucial if a lack of impulse and attention control characterizes ADHD. The ground-breaking 2006 study by Arthur Kramer, Ph.D., of the University of Illinois, showed via MRI scans that older persons' prefrontal brain volume grew with as little as three days of walking per week for six months.

And when Kramer examined several components of their executive function, the participants displayed enhanced working memory, fluid task switching, and the ability to filter out irrelevant inputs. Kramer wasn't looking for evidence of ADHD, but his findings show another way that exercise can be beneficial.

Everyone agrees that physical activity raises dopamine and norepinephrine levels. Amy Arnsten, Ph.D., a neurobiologist at Yale University, claims that one of these neurotransmitters' intracellular actions is to increase the prefrontal cortex's signal-to-noise ratio. Arnsten discovered that while dopamine lessens the noise or static of undirected neuron chatter, norepinephrine enhances the signal quality of synaptic transmission. As a result, the receiving cell is shielded from processing unnecessary signals.

The upside-down U pattern of neurotransmitter levels, according to Arnsten, means that raising them temporarily improves symptoms before having an adverse effect. The neurological soup requires maintenance at optimal levels, just like every other area of the brain, and exercise is the best recipe.

SWEAT STRATEGIES
To help patients manage their symptoms and medications, I recommend exercise to most of my patients. The optimum approach is to work out in the morning and then take the prescription an hour later when the exercise's immediate effects on concentration wane. I've discovered that everyday exercise helps some patients who need less stimulant medication.

I make an effort to work out first thing in the morning to give the day some structure and establish a positive mood, and that gives me motivation a lot of the time. Although the dopamine and norepinephrine surge duration following an exercise session has not been studied, anecdotal evidence points to an hour or even 90 minutes of calm and clarity. I advise those who require medicine to take it as soon as the effects of exercise start to wane to maximize the advantages of both strategies.

Everyone has a different degree of attention deficiency; therefore, they should try different strategies to determine what works for them. Knowing how it functions should help someone choose the best answer for themselves, in my opinion. I think the recommended amount of aerobic activity per day is 30 minutes. Given that it will enable one to focus sufficiently to make the most of the remaining hours of their day, it is not a significant amount of time.

HOW TO USE MINDFULNESS FOR WOMEN WITH ADHD

Katie Hamann's attention deficit hyperactivity disorder (ADHD) symptoms, such as inattention and feelings of distraction, were controlled with medication. She believed there was still more she could do to support herself as she dealt with her health.

Hamann, a 38-year-old who needed help with organization and time management, began visiting a therapist three years ago.

She claims that having children "threw a curveball in my time management system." "I needed aid because I could no longer manage by myself."

THE VALUE OF TREATMENT

The most efficient method for treating ADHD in adults seems to be a mix of medication, skill development, and counseling.

According to research, adults with ADHD who receive treatment that combines medication and cognitive behavioral therapy, a type of talk therapy aimed at altering thought and behavior patterns, are better able to control their symptoms than those who receive only medication. Self-esteem and organizational abilities also tend to advance.

Hamann underwent CBT for three months. Her therapist-assisted her in reducing self-critical thoughts and raising her self-esteem during their sessions. She also received organizing advice to assist her in creating project timetables.

According to John Mitchell, Ph.D., assistant professor in the Duke ADHD Program at Duke University Medical Center, "there are behavioral skills that individuals with ADHD don't employ as often or as successfully as adults without ADHD." "CBT aids in acquiring new behaviors and understanding how to practice them over time until they become habits regularly."

CHOOSING THE BEST FIT

You can get a therapy recommendation from your family doctor. Although there are therapists who focus on CBT for adults with ADHD, Mitchell acknowledges that finding one could be challenging.

As per Hamann, communication is essential.

She advises that you talk to someone with whom you feel at ease.

Additionally, insurance might not pay the bill. One recent study indicated that 15% of those persons must pay more than $200 out of pocket for mental health services and that 1 in 4 people do not have a mental health practitioner in their insurance network.

Consider a Team Approach Group therapy may be more accessible and economical than individual therapy.

According to J. Russell Ramsay, Ph.D., assistant professor at the University of Pennsylvania and co-founder and co-director of the Adult ADHD Treatment and Research Program, "groups can be highly targeted in addressing the issues encountered with ADHD and the coping mechanisms."

According to the participant, being in a program with other adults who have gone through similar experiences and being in a room with them is anadvantageof group therapy.

Group treatment can help with the toll ADHD can take on a couple's relationships. Consider seeing a marital and family therapist if your relationships suffer from ADHD symptoms, including impulsivity, inattention, and breaking commitments.

Invite the coach in

Even coaches for ADHD exist. They adopt a practical approach, providing planning, time management, and goal-setting tools to individuals with ADHD.

Ramsay claims that while ADHD coaches are not certified mental health specialists, working with one as a supplement to therapy might be beneficial.

Control Things Mindfully

Even with successful therapy or coaching, it's crucial to incorporate stress-reduction strategies like mindfulness meditation into your treatment plan. According to Mitchell's research, adults with ADHD who participated in an 8-week mindfulness meditation program reported improving their symptoms.

Mitchell acknowledges that persons with ADHD may find it difficult to maintain focus and stay still for a 30-minute meditation. Look for shorter, more energetic, and designed for people with ADHD, such as a 5-minute walking meditation.

According to him, mindfulness meditation is a great complement to CBT for people with ADHD. It alters your internal dialogue and teaches you to let go of criticism in favor of radical acceptance.

You can develop the skills required to thrive with ADHD with the correct therapist and therapeutic approach.

ADULT ADHD COGNITIVE BEHAVIORAL THERAPY

You presumably take medication to treat your symptoms if you have ADHD. Meds, however, don't always work, and cognitive behavioral therapy (CBT) can help with this. It can support you in overcoming obstacles in your relationships, career, and academic life.

CBT can help you feel better and ease daily life, whether you take medication or not.

WHAT CBT DOES

CBT is based on the notion that many issues begin with erroneous or negative beliefs.

Fox illustration

- I've made mistakes before, so I'll continue to do so.
- I'm not good in anyone's eyes.
- Everything that could go wrong will.
- Even minor issues are significant.
- The situation ought to be improved.
- I'm likely to lose my job since I don't enjoy it.
- Never will I measure up to my close friends, coworkers, partners, or husband.

CBT aids in your understanding of how negative thoughts cause challenges in your life. You discover how to swap out these false beliefs with genuine ones. The tasks you want and need to achieve are easier when you have an optimistic mindset. You get happier, feel better about yourself, and accomplish more things; as a result, creating a circle.

WHAT IT DOES

You and your doctor would discuss what you want to work on during the first few sessions. These are typically issues you deal with daily, and you might want to develop your planning, time management, or project completion skills, for instance.

To achieve your objectives, you will decide on an action plan. Between sessions, expect to complete some homework. You can use it to exercise your new abilities in real situations.

If you frequently arrive late, your therapist can advise you to wear a watch and install clocks in each room of your home. It's almost clear that this will increase your awareness of time, but it's also critical to determine whether or not your thoughts are contributing. Maybe you believe that no one expects you to be on time because you are constantly late; however, that is untrue. And you may alter the notion.

According to experts, those who have ADHD frequently "put out flames." CBT aims to alter your behavior and ideas so that the "fires" never ignite.

It's crucial to remember that CBT is among the finest remedies for anxiety and despair, two prevalent issues in individuals with ADHD.

LENGTH OF TIME

After 12 to 15 sessions or roughly three to four months, most people experience improvement. But you might want to stay a little longer, and it's simpler to form new behaviors when you receive more therapy time.

FINDING A THERAPIST

Not all therapists who treat ADHD employ CBT. Obtain a current list of therapists from your insurance provider as a starting point. Then inquire if your doctors have any recommendations from the list.

You might also like to

Ask for recommendations by calling a neighboring hospital or college psychology department.

Asking for advice from friends and family is nothing to be ashamed of.

Ask inquiries once you've located a therapist. Make certain they know about ADHD and need to fit you well. The treatment might not be as beneficial if you don't get along.

MEDS VS. CBT

Many patients discover they respond best to both medications and CBT. However, you may not wish to take medication or dislike its negative effects. CBT might therefore be effective on its own. Consult your doctor about it.

ADHD COACHING TIP

For some strange reason, ADHD has a reputation for being a life sentence for those who struggle with symptoms of inattention, hyperactivity, and impulsivity. That is frequently only the tip of the iceberg and is simply untrue. There are frequently many other aspects of a person's life that they are connected to when they are attempting to control their ADHD symptoms.

First off, there is no difference in the likelihood that someone with ADHD would succeed in life. Although you or your child may have difficulty finding or achieving success, you have the tools and resources to do whatever you desire.

While many people would have you believe that having ADHD is a surefire way to live in frustration and struggle, the truth is that whether we succeed or fail depends more on our actions and perspective. Here are three more methods to persist if you want to make things more difficult for yourself.

1. **Evaluate yourself against others.**

Constantly comparing yourself to others is one method to keep yourself upset and from achieving the success you want. Instead of focusing on what makes you special regarding your skills, consider where you fall short compared to others.

Never mind the unique conditions surrounding how long someone worked for success. If you keep telling yourself that you will never be good enough, you will inevitably struggle and become frustrated over and over again.

Spend more time contrasting who you are today with who you were yesterday if you want to succeed.

2. **Have Faith In Everyone.**

There are a lot of myths, rumors, and general rubbish going around concerning ADHD and how it might affect a person's life. It seems simpler to believe everyone and everything that comes our way to ask questions and try to figure things out for ourselves.

You increase your chances of struggling on the road to success by relying on the information of others without verifying their origins or authenticity. You keep looking for faults and difficulties to hold you back rather than learning from the mistakes others have made before you.

3. **One Measurement Fits Everybody.**

Nothing is more damaging than accepting generic advice and believing it to be true for you. This goes hand in hand with evaluating yourself concerning other people and taking everyone at their word. You will continue to have the same status as everyone else because of the one-size-fits-all mentality.

It would be okay if you focused more on determining what will work for you to succeed and develop original strategies for dealing with your symptoms and daily problems.

Attention deficit disorder is not a one-size fits all diagnosis. To effectively manage your or your child's ADHD symptoms, you must identify specific obstacles and solutions.

HOW TO MANAGE THE RELATIONSHIP FOR WOMEN WITH ADHD

Marriage and other relationships might suffer from ADHD. Due to the illness, it is challenging to recall social obligations, birthdays, or anniversaries, complete home tasks, and make timely payments on bills. Adults with ADHD may act recklessly or lose their anger easily. As a result, divorce and separation rates rise.

Compared to males with ADHD, women with ADHD have more difficulty interacting with others.

Women frequently feel overburdened by the obligations of relationships and hence have fewer fulfilling relationships. They struggle to maintain friendships and hardly ever start them, and isolation relieves suffering and perplexity.

They frequently experience rejection sensitivity, a strong emotional reaction to actual or perceived rejection that can make social engagement painful.

Compared to women without ADHD, they are more prone to engage in dangerous sexual practices. One explanation is that early sexuality acknowledgment quickly cuts to societal acceptance. In women with ADHD, it's typical to find a history of early sexual activity initiation, early sexual intercourse, more sexual partners, more casual sex, less protected sex, more STDs, and more unplanned pregnancies. These experiences are typical symptoms of ADHD, but they often cause embarrassment.

Your most essential relationship may fall apart due to attention deficit hyperactivity disorder. Distraction, procrastination, and other ADHD symptoms can make the spouse and the person with ADHD angry, frustrated, and upset. But if you treat your spouse or partner well and take precautions against miscommunication, your marriage or relationship can flourish.

DISTRACTION

The key sign of ADHD is this. Your ADHD companion doesn't appear to pay attention when you speak to them or keeps breaking commitments. You feel undesired, unheard, and neglected. They can genuinely care about you but be preoccupied with the TV, the phone, or their thoughts and fail to express them.

TECHNIQUES FOR DISTRACTION
First, quietly express your feelings to your ADHD partner. Feelings that are suppressed might result in bitterness and rage. Set aside a time to speak to your partner face-to-face and without interruptions if discussions are a huge issue. Touching your conversation partner might be beneficial. Admit it if you have ADHD and begin to lose focus. Have your partner say what they said again. Reconnecting is more difficult if the talk drags on and your thoughts wander.

HYPERFOCUS
The opposite of distraction is this. It could be challenging to take your focus off of something when you're so invested in it. You cannot look up from your smartphone or force yourself to put down that brand-new bestseller. Being hyperfocused might boost productivity, and unchecked might make you feel that your loved one is less significant than whatever has captured your attention.

STRATEGIES FOR HYPERFOCUS
Avoid engaging in certain activities, such as crossword puzzles or online games, if you tend to become hyperfocused during them, especially when you need to interact with your partner or just before meals. Set timers and track how much time you spend on each task. When you become aware that you are hyper-focusing, get up or move to break your focus. Try not to take it personally if you are the spouse or the partner.

FORGETFULNESS
You blanked out on your date and left your hubby stranded at the restaurant. Perhaps you failed to pay your electric bill, which turned your power off. Your lover thinks they can't rely on you to do anything simple. You experience failure on both sides, and anger increases.

STRATEGIES FOR FORGETTING
Forgetting things and other signs of ADHD are not character defects. Don't lecture or characterize the action as impolite or insensitive. Likewise, don't assume your partner's place, which might make you both angry. Instead, assist them in remembering by working with your partner. Utilize a laptop or a smartphone's calendar or reminders.

DISORGANIZATION
The partner with ADHD might forego or abandon tasks and frequently lose vital papers or car keys. Disorganization can lead to stress, lost time, and financial waste. Additionally, it may result in nagging and make the other person feel in charge.

DISORGANIZATION TECHNIQUES
Be calm and discuss the problems. Look for fixes next. Perhaps the partner with ADHD can handle the housework and washing instead of handling the finances or setting up carpools. To avoid the chore wars, play to each person's advantage. Recognize that your ADHD partner may need to keep things in specific locations to stay organized.

IMPULSIVITY
Impulsivity is another characteristic of those with the hyperactive form of ADHD. They frequently take action without first considering it. Impulsive spending is one prevalent issue, and you can overspend on unnecessary items or charge all of your credit cards. Some people might engage in unsafe sexual behavior or drive recklessly. Or, they might casually utter offensive remarks at gatherings.

TECHNIQUES FOR IMPULSIVITY
Learning self-control is possible. You can assist your partner in role-playing appropriate social behavior. Or the best way to wait one's turn. Bring money and stick to your shopping list if you tend to overspend. Eliminate temptations. Throw away catalogs and unsubscribe from emails from merchants. You might want assistance from an ADHD-trained therapist if impulsive behaviors become out of control.

PROCRASTINATION
We all put off doing difficult or dull things occasionally. But procrastination poses a significant challenge for people living with certain ADHD. You can feel overwhelmed by a project or have no idea where to begin, and last-minute deadlines can be what motivate you. That will result in a chaotic lifestyle that will be difficult for you and your partner.

PROCRASTINATION TECHNIQUES

If you divide a task into manageable pieces, you can complete it more quickly. Before completing step one, focus solely on the first portion. If you are the partner, see if you can split the work to assist. But be careful not to assume control over them. Most importantly, consider procrastination a trait that can be controlled rather than a personal flaw.

MOOD SWINGS
Emotional management is frequently difficult for those with ADHD. You could snap at someone or experience abrupt or significant mood swings. That's because you experience joy and happiness as well as anxiety and frustration more strongly than others, which might make your partner uncomfortable.

TECHNIQUES FOR MOOD SWING
Mood swings can be avoided with a balanced diet, sufficient sleep, and frequent exercise.
You can reduce tension and learn impulse control by doing yoga or tai chi.
Reactions should not be overreacted if you are the spouse. Instead, express empathy while also describing how they impact you. Take a hike or engage in an activity together.

ADHD IN CHILDREN AND RELATIONSHIPS
Not all children with ADHD have social interaction issues. You can take action to help your child's connections and social skills develop if they do. The more effectively such measures may be used, the earlier your child's issues with peers are addressed. You can help by:
Understanding the significance of positive peer relationships

Engage your child in activities with their peers; letting them participate in something they excel at or enjoy will give them the self-assurance to concentrate more on interacting with peers.

Together with your child, create social conduct objectives and a rewards system.

If your youngster is reclusive or overly shy, encourage social contact. Before your child attends an event, discuss what to anticipate there and from them in general.

Try not to attempt too much at once. Select one or two bad habits to tackle at once.

Don't go too far. It's not necessary for your child to be a member of the popular clique at school or to have a large social circle, and the only close friendships they require can be one or two.

Find out from your child's teachers how their classes are doing. Clear up any disagreements with them and the guidance counselor to prevent friendships from being hampered.

Bullying can also target children with ADHD. Get ready. You should discuss with your child what to do if they are being taunted or picked on. Assure them that it is acceptable to notify you if they are being bullied.

HOW CAN PARENTS SUPPORT AN ADHD-AFFECTED TEEN?

ADHD impacts all facets of a teen's life. Talking directly with your teen should be your priority as a parent. Always be accepting and supportive. Discussing ADHD and its therapy with your child's pediatrician is another option.

You may assist your teen in managing ADHD by doing the following:

- Set boundaries, instructions, and expectations that are clear and consistent.
- Establish a regular program and limit interruptions.
- Support your teen in activities that will allow for personal success (sports, hobbies, or music lessons, for example).
- Encourage your teen's positive actions to raise their sense of self-worth.
- Reward virtuous conduct.
- Impose penalties for inappropriate behavior.
- Help your teen stay organized and on a schedule.
- Maintain a schedule for your family, including a consistent mealtime, wake-up time, and bedtime.

Set up a reminder system at home to assist your teen in staying on track and remembering due dates for assignments. Include playtime and homework in the timetable if necessary. Kids may benefit from having a calendar or list as a visual representation of their schedule and discussing this frequently with them.

Make sure your teen pays attention in class by working with their professors.

When disciplining your teen, be composed.

Lead by example. Although they don't always express it, teens greatly value and look up to adults.

Make sure your adolescent gets enough rest. Establish clear guidelines for TV, laptops, phones, video games, and other devices. Make sure to turn off each of these well before going to bed.

Put ordinary objects in order. Everything is in its place, and your child should keep it that way. Clothing, rucksacks, and school supplies fall under this category.

Make use of notebook and homework organizers. Make sure your child knows how essential it is to record assignments and bring home the required books. A checklist can ensure that things like textbooks, lunchboxes, and jackets are carried home daily.

ONCE YOUR CHILD HAS GROWN

Maintaining your treatment schedule is key to living well with ADHD. Please encourage your child to consult with an ADHD specialist when they are adults. They should discuss how to take their medications on their own as a group. If they receive talk therapy, they should also have a strategy for keeping up with it.

Talk about how they can order fresh medication before the old one expires. Make sure they have a new doctor or ADHD specialist close to their new home if they are moving away or leaving for school so they can obtain care when they need it.

Your child has to understand the significance of taking their medication exactly as directed by their doctor. They will experience worsening symptoms if not. This can make it challenging to learn or perform successfully at work and even increase the likelihood that they'll engage in harmful behavior, like abusing alcohol.

Make sure they know they should never give anybody else their prescriptions.

Additionally, it would help if you discussed with your child the everyday obligations of living alone. How will they prepare meals and wash laundry, for instance? Which bills should they anticipate paying, and how?

SET LIMITATIONS.

Regardless of their ADHD, treating your child like an adult is important in assisting them in being self-reliant. If they don't want aid, respect their privacy and don't bother them about what they should be doing. You might also want to act in a way that demonstrates to them that you are treating them like adults. You may, for instance, invite them to dinner rather than drop by their flat unannounced.

Planning with your kid is an excellent idea. Let them know that you are accessible if they need you. For instance, they might want you to remind them each month that their rent is due. Verify that your youngster is making the requests, though.

PUT THE EXPERTS TO WORK.

You might be accustomed to assisting your child in many facets, such as money management and navigating challenging social situations. Even though they are adults, you should continue to show them love and support. But encouraging them to ask for help from others is one way to assist them in transitioning to adulthood. For instance, a life coach with expertise in ADHD can assist them in improving their study techniques. When dealing with conflict, a therapist can also assist them in finding constructive communication methods.

HOW TO MANAGE WORK FOR WOMEN WITH ADHD

Keeping a job can be challenging for those with ADHD. They frequently struggle to prioritize tasks, follow instructions, maintain organization, and meet deadlines. Additionally, they frequently arrive late and make sloppy errors. Only 50% of persons with ADHD had full-time jobs in one nationwide study, compared to 72% of adults without the disease. Those with ADHD typically make less money than their counterparts.

The occupations where people with ADHD are likely to succeed are not well studied. However, according to Dr. Russell A. Barkely, an expert in ADHD, his patients have achieved success in various trade jobs such as sales, acting, the military, photography, and coaching sports. A person with ADHD is capable of pursuing practically any line of work.

ADHD JOB COACHING

Coaching or mentorship may help people with ADHD improve their performance at work. The mentor will advise on prioritizing a to-do list, taking notes, and keeping a daily planner. It might be beneficial to work in a distraction-free environment. The Americans with Disabilities Act recognizes ADHD as a disability, meaning that firms must alter their practices to accommodate a worker's needs.

Many women with ADHD experience being overwhelmed, rushing to accomplish tasks at the last minute and feeling disorganized and irritated when they can't get everything on their "to-do" list.

Most adults will identify negatively as "procrastinators" when they exhibit these typical ADHD tendencies. Others identify themselves as " time optimists."

You have to plan your day full of "things to do confidently," so when you consistently find yourself running late for appointments, work, bedtime, or other commitments or deadlines that weren't completed, assume you need more time.

It's crucial to understand whether you procrastinate (delay tasks until the last minute) or you are a "time optimist" (underestimate the amount of time you have to complete tasks). The approaching deadline serves as our driving force when we put something off. Conversely, the "time optimist" frequently underestimates the time required to complete daily tasks.

Most individuals are unaware that adult ADHD frequently manifests as a lack of "time awareness." The incapacity to predict how long a task will take to finish is among its manifestations. For example, we might schedule a half-hour trip to work but fail to account for the extra time required to leave the house, parking, and slow elevators. As a result, you rush to work, arrive late, and feel overburdened. Adults with ADHD who struggle with "time awareness" may find it difficult to recognize the passing of time. For instance, 2 hours can seem like 5 minutes, and 5 minutes can seem like 2 hours. We sit down to respond to that one email before we leave the house, but 20 minutes later, we're rushing to the office, running late once more and unsure of how the time passed.

People with ADHD who are typically clever even report having trouble remembering the days of the week, the months of the year, or the year's seasons in sequence. Some adults with ADHD report that it impairs their memory of specific times.

The first step is realizing that this is just one of many difficulties that ADHD might present in our daily life. Keeping a journal of when and how long it takes us to perform daily duties for a couple of weeks is a tremendous eye-opener for many "time optimists." We frequently underestimate the time it will take to complete a task and end up feeling upset because we couldn't get more done. What most people learn after doing this exercise is that it would take a miracle of a 27-hour day to do everything on their list that they first believed they could or "should" complete in a day. Finding out how long some of your "to-do's" REALLY take to accomplish will help you arrange your day more "time realistic." Your "to-do list" will be manageable and realistic, so frustration won't increase from being overloaded.

Utilizing what I refer to as "external" reminders is another method for helping ADHD individuals who struggle with "time awareness." In essence, clocks are everywhere! Even better are alarm clocks and timers. Use analog clocks in your home and place of business, set phone alarms, and wear a watch with a timer. Having all these reminders appears to help the most with keeping track of time, knowing how long something truly takes to do and developing a realistic plan.

HOW TO MANAGE MONEY FOR WOMEN WITH ADHD

When you have ADHD, managing money might be difficult, but it's a crucial skill. Once you develop your financial strategy, you can discover that you can control it. Consider how free it would be to be organized: You wouldn't have to worry about your bank account dropping abruptly, getting denied for a loan, or having your power turned off because you forgot to pay the bill.

YOUR FINANCIAL RELATIONSHIP
Issues with the following may make managing finances more challenging for persons with ADHD:
- Keeping an eye on your money balance or spending
- Keeping track of cheques, bills, and crucial tax documents to prevent late payments
- spending and significant credit card debt
- putting off · putting off cleaning files or paying payments
- saving for upcoming demands or desires
- Be aware of your financial activities.

Keeping track of your purchases can help you rein in reckless spending, and you may also check where your money is going with its assistance. Keep track of your purchases, no matter how tiny, in a compact notepad you carry or with a smartphone app that suits your needs. Include any online purchases or payments you make as well. As you keep track of your spending, specific categories will become apparent. These could include food, entertainment, snacks, coffee shops, books, movies, gas, transportation costs, clothing, newspapers, cosmetics, home goods, charitable contributions, and hobbies.

Tracking your expenditures may seem difficult or bothersome initially, but it persists, even if only for a few weeks. To compare notes, if you're married or in a partnership, your spouse or partner should also keep track of their spending. If you're single, you might ask a close friend or relative to check in on you periodically to ensure you're still on track. Even if you don't record every expense perfectly, the data you gather will help you develop better money management practices. In your tracking, take into account both fixed and variable expenses.

Housing, utilities, loans, and transportation are all fixed costs.

Consumable costs include food, gas, clothing, and entertainment (an average amount or range)

Taxes, homeowner association dues, and memberships should be considered when calculating monthly, quarterly, and annual expenses.

Your fixed and variable costs are combined. You must reevaluate your expenses to determine where you can make savings or eliminate expenses if they exceed your income. Your disposable income is the money that remains after those outgoing costs. What you choose to do with your extra cash will depend on your circumstances and preferred way of living. You may use it for things like eating, house renovations or repairs, trips, classes, retirement savings, etc.

CONSIDER YOUR PRINCIPLES AND OBJECTIVES.

Spend some time thinking about your immediate and long-term objectives. You should discuss your goals with your spouse or partner if you have one.

Making a collage of a few items you want to save for or making notes about them might be useful. Sort your list of images into two categories: necessary (for safety, security, or well-being) and not necessary (would like to have). What three to five items top your list of necessities? Your list of unnecessary items? What stands in the way of where you are and want to be? You can establish financial savings or spending goals after clarifying your vision and locating any issue areas.

Short-term objectives can include setting aside a particular weekly amount, cutting back on eating out, or maintaining organization in your financial records.

Mid-term objectives could include paying off a little debt, such as a store charge card, or saving for a trip or a new piece of furniture.

Long-term objectives could include retirement preparation or college tuition savings.

Your goals can be broken down into manageable action steps that you can take daily, weekly, monthly, or annually. If you need assistance, don't hesitate to approach a friend, therapist, or coach. Keep in mind that effective money management requires being mindful of all of your objectives. They are a crucial component of your daily financial regimen.

HOW TO IMPROVE FOCUS IN WOMEN WITH ADHD

Most people would probably describe a frantic child running around the room, wrecking everything if asked to describe a child with ADHD based on the term alone. Although not unusual, this is one example of a child's behavior, which can vary widely. The disease may cause some kids to become introverted and very quiet.

Inattention, hyperactivity, and impulsivity are the three main signs of ADHD; therefore, these symptoms will most likely affect how the child behaves in public. One of your children might be inattentive but neither hyperactive nor impulsive, while another might exhibit all three behaviors (most common).

The terrible part for any child who does not exhibit impulsive or hyperactive behavior is that they frequently go unnoticed. They are overlooked because they aren't always "acting up," even if their demand for attention is just as great. Children who struggle with attention will suffer academically and socially if they are not diagnosed promptly.

FOCUSING TECHNIQUES FOR ADULTS WITH ADHD
1. **Reduce Your Field Of Vision**

Keep only what you're working on in front of you at your workstation while you're there. Remove anything else from your field of vision.

2. **Write A Letter To Yourself**

If you need to focus for a few hours on a research paper, jot down a note and put it somewhere you can see it:

"Cleaning my room now is not the right moment. Tomorrow, I can complete that. This is merely the preliminary version, and it is not necessary to use precise grammar and language.

3. **Avoid Being Critical.**

Before you finish, wait to offer feedback on your work. You'll be able to avoid becoming bogged down by perfectionism or feeling frustrated by how much work still has to be done.

4. **Create A List.**

Take five minutes to jot out the work if a flurry of worries keeps you from focusing on it. You'll find it simpler to focus after these chores are written down, and you're not worried about remembering everything.

5. **Request A Polite Reminder**

In meetings or classes, when you share a seat with a friend, confide in them. Ask them to tap you on the shoulder if you seem to be drifting off.

6. Exercise Frequently.

The best method to encourage long-term focus is through it. More oxygen is delivered to the brain during exercise, which also triggers the release of nutrients, hormones, neurotransmitters, and other substances that improve brain function.

7. Know Your Limitations.

Be honest when you are straying and can no longer concentrate on listening. Say "I'm sorry" to the individual you're speaking to. Can we pause for a moment? I can't concentrate because my medication is gone.

8. Set A Target.

You'll go to great lengths to stay on task and complete the task at hand if your goal aligns with who you are and what you're passionate about.

STIGMA IN WOMEN WITH ADHD

Sex conventions may compel girls to cover up and hide ADHD symptoms. Girls and women may be influenced by stereotypes about collaboration, compliance, neatness, and social behaviors to hide or mask their ADHD symptoms at home and school.

According to a 2019 study, teachers may struggle to identify ADHD symptoms in girls because of sex disparities. Healthcare professionals may be less likely to diagnose girls with ADHD unless they also exhibit indications of emotional issues because the symptoms can be milder in girls.Medical providers may be more likely to treat girls' anxiety and despair without identifying concomitant ADHD, claims a 2014 research review.

Girls with attention deficit are perceived as "emotional" or "difficult" since they frequently lack the accompanying hyperactivity. When hyperactivity is considered, many refer to them as tomboys or flaky or flighty. Due to their emotional outbursts, these females also get into more confrontations with their peers, but nobody ever realizes that they have ADHD.

It's fascinating that while females exhibit many of the same attention deficit symptoms as men, such as disorganization, impulsivity, and problems with time management, some girls don't even have this trait until they are adults. Usually, when their kids are diagnosed, they are.By that point, she is an adult ADHD woman, and many of the symptoms, whether or not a physician recognizes them, cause her more distress. How come? Because superwoman multitasking is frequently modeled for girls.

Women, in general, believe that to succeed in business, they must be twice as good as males. Due to her impulsivity and focus challenges, this expectation can cause a woman with adult ADHD to experience excruciating anxiety. Although it is unrealistic for women to believe that society expects them to be flawless, adult women with ADHD may experience depression and low self-esteem because no one can be flawless, especially those with ADHD.

This is typically seen in the adult ADHD woman's home. The area is congested, and the TV can have two inches of dust on it, like in the aftermath of an aviation crash. It's a mess! And as a result, she declines invitations to parties. She may even experience additional anxiety, guilt, and shame at the mere prospect of someone approaching the door and observing her inflated mess.

There is additional stress when adult ADHD women must work outside the home, and they must arrive at work on time and complete their tasks satisfactorily. She also has to worry about picking up groceries, dropping off cleaning, doing laundry, cooking, and all the other responsibilities that come with being a mother, which adds to her already heavy workload. This can be very challenging because of her inability to organize herself and manage her time well. However, that is only true in the case of a complete family, a two-parent home. What transpires when an adult ADHD woman experiences a divorce, which is very likely in adult ADHD relationships? She is now responsible for her other partner's responsibilities, job, and domestic obligations. She is responsible for handling everything about the house. What does she do if the water heater breaks or the roof leaks? She'll handle it like any other adult, but when she's expected to do so much, it can be terrible, especially when these pressures on the adult ADHD woman aren't simply external.

Menstruation and menopause are internal bodily processes that might cause emotional ups and downs. Additionally, attention deficit can worsen all of the symptoms a woman has during these periods of her life. Fortunately, some women can control their ADHD symptoms by reaching adulthood. While some people may still have a full-blown attention deficit, others may have one or two symptoms. However, if these symptoms worsen and are left untreated, they can result in the negative effects of ADD, such as addiction, despair, and an all-around terrible life. Concentrate on the positive aspects of having attention deficit disorder, such as your creativity and excitement. If your symptoms are too bad, though, get medical attention. Do not let adult ADD cause you to be unhappy; it just isn't necessary.

GETTING PAST THE STIGMA OF ADHD
Being diagnosed with ADHD or having a child with the disease are neither improper nor embarrassing. That is, at least, the ideal situation. However, there are many different viewpoints about ADHD and persons who have it. Even though there is evidence to suggest they are just as competent, skillful, and creative as "normal" people, children and adults who are diagnosed with the illness are considered "defective" or "deviant." How may the stereotype of ADHD be reduced? How can you guard against discrimination or ridicule for your child? Here are some responses.
ADHD STIGMATIZATION

Many individuals still do not think that ADHD is a real medical illness, despite all the studies and media coverage it has gotten. Instead, they see it as a justification for lazy behavior or poor parenting. The fact that the severity of the symptoms varies depending on the circumstance only strengthens the doubts of the skeptics. Why can't your child concentrate on academics when he can spend hours playing video games, for example, is what they'll remark. The stigma is exacerbated by the fact that ADHD affects one's ability to function well at work or school. These are the criteria by which our society determines a person's value, and youngsters with poor grades or adults with low job ratings are frequently denigrated.

THE INJURY
Workplace discrimination and social issues are the most overt effects of the stigma surrounding ADHD. While kids with ADHD are more prone to experience bullying, adults with ADHD may experience employment rejection after disclosing their diagnosis.

However, the worst harm occurs when the person with ADHD internalizes these unfavorable perceptions. For instance, it's fairly usual for kids with ADHD to tell me that they stopped going to school because they're just not good enough for it or that they're frightened to attempt new things because they think they're not good enough. They no longer strive to change their behavior and succeed since the stigma associated with ADHD has negatively impacted their motivation and sense of self.

ADHD STIGMA VICTIMS
Everyone with ADHD has dealt with the stigma at some point, but girls and young women bear the stigma most heavily. Most people still believe that boys only experience the symptoms of ADHD; therefore, girls and women who exhibit daydreaming, disorganization, or forgetfulness must have a serious mental illness. Adults are subject to the same kinds of stereotypes. Due to the widespread misconception that ADHD is a childhood condition, adults who claim to have it are sometimes viewed with skepticism. People tend to think that adults with ADHD are merely making up reasons for their failings rather than having a real problem.

HOW CAN YOU HELP?

What you can do to help someone with ADHD or a child who has it is to spread knowledge of it, especially among skeptics. When someone makes a derogatory comment regarding ADHD, you should gently but firmly address this stereotype. You may demonstrate how your child struggles to perform better in school despite the symptoms or explain why ADHD is just as real as diabetes or asthma.

LIVING WITH A WOMAN DIAGNOSED WITH ADHD

A true disorder having a neurological foundation is ADHD. It affects around 5% of the American population, making it a real issue for many people. Please stop trying to disprove it or use it as a justification. With the right interventions, it is a condition that can be managed, helped, improved upon, and surpassed.

If you have ADHD, you could occasionally feel like your spouse is annoyed by your conduct, but you might not know why or how to make them feel better. Although each person is unique, some typical behaviors might cause conflict, such as being disorganized or forgetful or blurting out your opinions. Recognize the flashpoints and learn what you can do to reduce the stress.

WHEN DISORDER CAUSES CONFLICT

Christine Cox, a producer who resides in New York City with her ADHD-afflicted husband Max, a professional magician, declares that she is "a planner and organizer, always thinking ahead." Because of her meticulous planning, Christine organizes and promotes Max's magic act.

The opposite is true of Max, which is excellent for him but bad for her. "My husband has spent his entire life surrounded by commotion. Chaos, meantime, is a trigger for me."

According to Sharon Saline, PsyD, a psychologist with expertise in ADHD, this is typical. According to her, "many couples with ADHD have conflicting ideals of cleanliness and organization." Both parties might become angry as a result.

STEPS TO TAKE.

Make a list of the triggers or issue locations each of you sees. Choose one and get to work on it. To increase organization, develop a system. Saline speculates that the organization may use color labeling or distinct compartments sorted alphabetically.

WHEN DISPUTES RELATE TO WHO DOES WHAT CHORES

Teri Schroeder, a therapist who co-owns the Just Mind counseling center in Austin, Texas, with her husband William, a therapist with ADHD, says she sometimes feels that she must bear an unfair share of the burden of home duties.

William does not think to take command, so Teri does. Nothing gets done without her cooperation. She explains, "I have to oversee and assign everything."

According to Chad Perman, a licensed marriage and family therapist in Bellevue, WA, this is typical in relationships impacted by ADHD. Because they are considerably more organized, dependable, and capable of finishing things quickly, the non-ADHD partner frequently handlesmuch housework and parenting.

You can be in a "parent-child relationship," where your significant other feels forced to play the part of the responsible "parent," and you unintentionally take on the character of the carefree "kid." Both of you might find it frustrating.

STEPS TO TAKE.

Work on a plan with a partner. Decide on the exact tasks you will be in charge of. Set reminders on your phone to ensure that you remember to do things.

WHEN YOU FORGET IMPORTANT INFORMATION

According to Teri Schroeder, forgetfulness can be frustrating. "I occasionally send William to Trader Joe's to pick up two items, and he then takes longer and only returns with one of the products."

She will dismiss a minor issue and may even joke about it, which is beneficial. When she worries that he could forget to feed the cats while she is out of town or that the dog would run out of water, she says, "It's less humorous."

Max Cox is aware that his forgetfulness and inattentiveness can be an issue. He says I might promise to mail something for my wife but fail to do it on time or fail to remember.

He regrets not honoring his promise. He says, "She ought to be able to depend on me. "Trusting someone you can't depend on is difficult, and to doubt your spouse's loyalty mustache."

STEPS TO TAKE.

Make some lists. After finishing each item, strike through it. On your phone, set reminders and notifications.

HOW TO TELL IF YOUR PARTNER IS UNLOVED

Your partner might assume you don't care if you overlook their requirements or forget about things that are significant to them. Ned Hallowell, MD, a psychiatrist and prominent international speaker on

ADHD, argues that "this is fairly typical in relationships affected by ADHD." He claims that although the cause is neurological, it's frequently misunderstood as a lack of affection.

Teri Schroeder experiences this when William isn't present. She claims that occasionally he walks too quickly and becomes disoriented and forgetful, losing track of where she is.

He frequently loses track of me if we go to a pub and he runs into friends. He might not notice if I need a drink or get caught in a crowd. She understands it's not on purpose, but she still gets the impression that he doesn't give a damn.

William says, "I hate that this happened to her since it doesn't reflect my intentions." He has too much on his plate, so he moves more quickly and misses some things.

STEPS TO TAKE.
Instead of criticizing or making the other feel defensive, William and Teri agree it helps to express oneself quietly. Then, William argues, "we can work through issues as a team." You might try mindfulness-enhancing activities as a partner with ADHD.

WHEN YOUR THOUGHTS BECOME BLURRED
How you interact with your relationship may be impacted by ADHD. You might speak without thinking, struggle to pay attention during a discussion, or interrupt.

According to Perman, "These actions are typically perceived as impolite, dismissive, or cruel by the non-ADHD spouse."

According to Saline, "many ADHD couples deal with emotional outbursts and heated disagreements."

STEPS TO TAKE.
Before you talk, pause. Whenever things get hot, take a break. After you've had time to calm down, reassemble it to discuss it.

Whatever the source of conflict, Perman advises couples to schedule time each week to practice active listening together. Plan a joint strategy for recurrent problems. When you can, find humor in the circumstance. When feelings begin to escalate, take a break. Concentrate on the qualities that are similar or excellent in each other.

PARENTING ADVICE FOR ADHD:

Although ADHD is not an excuse, it can potentially explain a child's behavior.

There are many misconceptions concerning ADHD, and many people believe that the condition is simply a means for some kids to get away with misbehavior.

I'm here to assure you that this is not the case personally. But I can also see how someone may think that way. Many individuals lack an understanding of ADHD and how it impacts a child.

Nothing is more perplexing and irritating for a parent of an ADHD child than trying to predict their child's conduct. This is one of the most frequent queries, and challenges parents encounter, as someone who works with families with children with ADHD can attest.

Why is my kid acting this way? Can I do anything to help? Will they ever understand?

ADHD is not, and never should be, a justification. It can, however, be a compelling justification for what is occurring.

I constantly advise parents to observe the behavior and consider the following: "Is this behavior acceptable?"

Once we know the answer, we can determine how to address the behavior and how ADHD affects that particular behavior.

REASON VS. DEFENSE

Now, realizing and accepting that ADHD is a genuine, biological disorder is the most crucial step. It is totally up to you whether you consider it a disorder, illness, or deficit. I won't use those words, though.

Instead, I want to emphasize the variations in the brain and the resulting variations in behavior. To me, having ADHD means having a different way of digesting, absorbing, and experiencing the world. That doesn't mean that people with ADHD don't face unique difficulties.

I'm not at all implying that. However, I firmly think that any behavior can be managed, controlled, molded, and learned. The challenging aspect is that.

Most individuals concentrate on the defining signs of impulsivity, hyperactivity, and inattention. Unfortunately, these only reflect what the ADHD child is experiencing. The difficulties stem from a lack of ability in time management, planning, organization, decision-making, working memory, and other associated "executive function"-related abilities.

Once we comprehend and accept this, we can let go of the notion that bad conduct is a symptom of ADHD and instead reflects on the very real obstacles young kids face, challenges they frequently encounter with little assistance and support.

The next time your child engages in conduct you don't approve of, you do not have to accept it, and you are not required to support them or anybody else by using the justification that "Oh, it's my child's ADHD."

Instead, you may now work with your child to become more conscious of how and when they become more impulsive, hyperactive, and inattentive since you know better. Now that you know the tasks and activities that trigger these behaviors, you can better understand how an ADHD child's intense frustration leads to them.

LIFE MANAGEMENT TOOLS FOR WOMEN WITH ADHD

Some persons with ADHD benefit from having a coach for daily life, similar to having a mentor at work. In general, coaching is used in addition to more formal psychological treatment. The mentor assists the patient in applying newly acquired abilities in practical contexts, such as organizing the home or making travel plans.

For those with ADHD, smartphone "organizer" apps can be extremely helpful. You may always have a new to-do list by using an app to make one every night. Use the four categories of calls, emails, tasks, and errands to keep your list organized. You may avoid missing key occasions by keeping your itinerary current with other apps.

If you're a woman with ADHD, you could find it difficult to handle situations that others seem to handle in a flash. Have you burned your cakes? Or perhaps you forgot to tidy the kitchen after breakfast until it was time for dinner. You didn't think about the silly dishes because you focused intently on a project. You are not alone, though. Even if that might bring some solace, some of you feel hopeless and depressed.

Stop that from happening! When you have ADHD, you can utilize various strategies to help things move more easily for you. Let's use a dinner party to demonstrate how someone with ADHD may organize everything.

First, divide things into manageable pieces to make things easier for your ADHD to handle.

If you frequently forget that items are cooking, the cooking itself can be frightening. Place timers! This is quite significant. If your appliances don't already have them built in, buy a few timers and set one for each course you're cooking. Modern equipment typically comes with them already built in. The dish that takes the longest to prepare should be the first course you serve. Therefore, you should set the first timer if you're cooking something that needs three or four hours, like a turkey.

Use whichever many you need, one for what is in the microwave and one for what is on the burner. And make sure they keep ringing so your ADHD brain won't be able to ignore them and forget. Please make sure they are loud enough for you to hear in case you are in the adjacent room.

Of course, cooking is just one aspect of the situation; you must also consider cleaning your home. You want visitors to feel at ease. Okay, then divide that up into reasonable portions for ADHD. Determine how much time you have before the party and how many tasks you must complete. Determine how long you can keep up with housework before becoming bored due to ADHD. Decide how much time you'll need for each task after that. As a result, dusting will take an hour, vacuuming a half-hour, and organizing and putting everything away will take three hours. You also have to clean the kitchen, the floors, and other things. If not, select how long you need for cleaning. You may have as many days as you need. If you can only clean for an hour at a time, require five hours to complete it, and have five days to finish it, that's excellent! You'll finish on schedule if you put in that hour every day.

However, if you only have three days and need five hours to clean your house, you might need to divide your time into two periods, one in the morning and one in the evening. Just be careful not to get bored by it to the point that you can't get back to it.

Sit down with your cookbook, some paper, and a pencil, and list everything you want to buy for your meal. Check what you have and what you need next. You make a list of all your needs. The key here is to keep in mind to bring the list with you to the grocery store. Please put it on a piece of paper with a vibrant color and tuck it inside your shoe, on top of your purse, or next to your car keys. It would help if you also put it using a pen or pencil. It can be placed wherever that it will be impossible to forget. Once you get to the grocery shop, you pull out your list and a pen and check off each item as you purchase it. This will assist your ADHD brain in remembering what you need to pick up while saving time.

These are fundamental actions that both men and women with ADHD can take, although ADHD women with families typically struggle to organize events like dinner parties. Finding ADHD-friendly solutions that work well for you is the key to success, and your life goes a lot more smoothly when you can accomplish that.

DAILY LIFE ADVICE FOR ADULTS WITH ADHD
   1. **Check Your Calendar Three Times A Day**

Organizing tips might help you better manage your time and activities, whether you have ADHD or have too much to remember. Make it a habit to schedule your events and activities on a calendar. It makes no difference if it's a desk calendar, a smartphone app, or anything else. Check it at least three times daily and keep it in one location. Establish a routine by checking at the same times every day.
   2. **Every Day, Create A New "To-Do" List.**

Make a list of the tasks you wish to accomplish each day in the morning. To increase your chances of finishing everything on your list, try to keep it as realistic as possible. Sort your jobs according to significance, starting with the most crucial ones. Give a fixed time of day to each assignment. When you finish a task, check it off your list.

3. Start By Organizing Each Room Individually.

Don't let the notion of "being organized" frighten you. Start by discarding unnecessary items and returning them to their proper places.

Take on each room one at a time, beginning with the simplest. If necessary, divide the space into separate areas.

In your planner, block off time for an organization. To control your work sessions, set a timer.

Consider if you want to keep or discard certain goods, and put them in a different box to review later if you're unsure.

4. Make It A Daily Habit To Be Organized

Could you not consider it to be cleaning? Consider it as adhering to your organizational plan:

If you keep things, give them a place to live. Utilize over-the-door organizers, filing cabinets, labels, and transparent storage containers. Spend 10 minutes each day picking up and putting things back where they belong.

Put something back if you took it out.

Keep a box for storing stray papers and other lost stuff. At the end of each day, go over it.

5. Keep Tiny Items Close Together.

Place a modest table or bookshelf next to your home's entrance. Place a tray or basket on top to hold vital goods like keys, wallets, watches, glasses, and phones. Additionally, you can utilize this space to store other goods like lunchboxes, briefcases, critical documents, or outgoing mail that you want to keep in mind.

6. Provide A Changing Menu

It could not be easy to organize regular family meals. Make a "Top 10" dinner list or a recurring menu of simple meals. Try to keep those ingredients on hand, or make a list on index cards you can carry. Have a "free" night where you order takeout or divide the cooking duties with other family members to avoid bearing the responsibility of feeding everyone.

7. Establish A Mail Schedule

Create a mechanism for daily mail inspection and sorting. One suggestion is to designate a specific space to store all vital mail, including checks, bills, insurance documents, and bank statements. At least once every week, go over this stack, putting invoices in a pile to be paid and other relevant papers in the correct folders. Remove your name from mailing lists to stop unwanted mail from reaching your home.

8. Keep A Record Of Your Spending.

For those with ADHD, managing money can be challenging, especially if you tend to buy things on impulse. Carry a notebook, utilize an electronic gadget, or visit a financial website to record every purchase you make, even the smallest ones. You can better manage your finances if you know how much and what you spend each month.

9. Utilize Digital Reminders

Forgetting appointments, due dates, prescriptions, or other obligations can lead to issues at work and in your personal life. Use computer programs and other electronic gadgets to assist you in remembering deadlines and appointments. Set your computer or smartphone, for instance, to notify you five minutes before each event in your calendar.

10. Distractions At Work: Tune Them Out

For adults with ADHD, distractions at work can be a major difficulty. Try the following tactics:

Send your calls to voicemail, and only listen to them during specific hours each day.

To avoid being interrupted at work, request a quiet office or cubicle.

Use earphones or a "white noise" machine to block out outside noise during work.

Limit yourself to completing one task at a time.

11. Defeat Boredom

Many persons with ADHD rapidly grow bored, especially when doing mundane jobs or paperwork. At work, it could be challenging to maintain concentration. Try the following advice:

Divide up larger jobs into smaller ones.

Walk or get some fresh air in between tasks.

During meetings, make notes.

12. Make Life Simpler By Doing Fewer Tasks

Your environment can be made more clutter-free, easier to keep track of your possessions, and less distracting by organizing and simplifying it.

Streamlining might benefit your schedule as well. Wait until you've completed the present project or assignment before beginning a new one. Try not to overload your schedule with too many jobs or projects at once. To maintain focus, you might need to practice turning down new activities.

13. Increase Your Exercise

Your symptoms of ADHD may be managed with regular exercise, and it can, at the very least, enable you to channel surplus energy. However, regular physical activity and team sports can also teach you how to collaborate with people, create and achieve goals, and feel better about yourself. According to certain studies, physical activity may stimulate brain regions linked to ADHD. Yoga and karate may be helpful for ADHD patients since they allow individuals to memorize moves.

14. Commence Work In 15-Minute Blocks

Try this exercise if you're having problems beginning a project:
Set a 15-minute timer.
Concentrate entirely on that one task for those 15 minutes.
When the allotted time has passed, consider if you can continue for an additional 15 minutes.
Try to reset the timer if you can. As long as you can, continue for 15 minutes at a time.
Stop and try again later or the next day if you cannot continue.

15. Employ Color Coding

You may maintain greater organization using colored notes, folders, and files. Here are a few illustrations:
Use color-coded folders to keep track of various expenses, including grocery, transportation, entertainment, and utilities.
To differentiate between obligations for business, personal, and family time, use different colored pens or highlighters in your planner.

16. Study Your To-Do Lists

Try to determine why there are so many undone items on your "to-do" lists. Did you attempt to complete everything at once? Did you include any large jobs that you could have divided into smaller ones? Or did you fail to finish your job because of distractions? Utilize this information to organize future "to-do" lists or identify more productive strategies.

SELF-LOVE FOR WOMEN WITH ADHD

It can be frustrating to have ADHD, and it can be exhausting to overcome the difficulties, so they don't interfere with daily functioning and pick up new skills. When managing ADHD, there is a constant internal conflict between your symptoms and coping mechanisms. There are many aspects of having ADHD that is draining, but having to put up with or listen to those who don't understand it or have preconceived notions about it has to be at the top of the list.

Children with ADHD often believe or hear that they are "too much," bothersome, slothful, unmotivated, not reaching their full potential, challenging, frustrating, or odd as they grow up. Adult with ADHD builds their identity and sense of self on these labels and relationships with others.

Henry David Thoreau once stated that what you see matters, not what you look at. Dr. Ned Hallowell advises families to look past the difficult ADHD symptoms and discover the "mirror qualities," or the beneficial features of the ADHD symptoms.

For instance, although many people with ADHD "appear" and act hyperactive, they might also be perceived as energized. A girl or woman can be "perceived" as persistent rather than being characterized as stubborn. A young man can be "perceived" as creative and spontaneous while also struggling with impulsivity. We can see various things in the mirror and our kids, depending on where we are.

Even when given an appropriate diagnosis and support, children and teens with ADHD generally get a lot of negative feedback as they negotiate school, activities, friendships, and family interactions. They are informed that they are "too much," unpleasant, unmotivated, lazy, not living up to their potential, difficult, frustrating, or weird by themselves or others.

Adult with ADHD builds their identity and sense of self on these labels and relationships with others. Every person must learn to appreciate, comprehend, and accept themselves, but adults with ADHD may need to work harder and be pushed to do so in a more concentrated and organized manner.

The easy steps listed below can assist anyone with ADHD in developing self-acceptance and self-love:

BE A KIND LISTENER.
Pay attention to how your ADHD affects you in both difficult and beneficial ways in your daily life. Use nonjudgmental language to help you observe yourself, your challenges, and your accomplishments. By developing your observational skills, you will

learn to notice and accept the many facets of who you are with less fear and shame.

EXAMINE YOUR OPINIONS AND ADJUST THE MIRROR.
Review the list of mirror features provided by Dr. Hallowell if you realize that you are identifying largely unfavorable and unpleasant aspects of yourself. Do you need to adjust the mirror so you can view yourself differently? Would a considerate friend or a family member have a different opinion of you or some of those ADHD traits?

PRACTICE SELF-LOVE AND ACCEPTANCE
It takes work and is not a quick remedy. You may have experienced various degrees of unfavorable criticism over your life. It won't be enough to read one self-help book, repeat mantras for one day, or learn the list of mirror attributes. You must put forth the effort each day to look for opportunities to recognize your abilities and yourself. The wiring of our minds is to evaluate the negative each day. As a novel experiment, note a few things you do each day that make you feel good, proud, or joyful. Instead of reading over the usual list of "what went wrong during the day," try reading through that list before bed.

TEACH OTHERS AND YOURSELF.
It is not necessarily your responsibility to educate others about ADHD and campaign for its acceptance. But you can choose your own story and how you show yourself to the world by being aware of your neurobiology and willing to put your actions in the context of your ADHD. By doing this, you might be able to avoid falling victim to the unkind interpretations and judgments of others and open the door to kinder and truer perceptions of both yourself and other people. And wouldn't we all benefit from a bit more sympathy and compassion?

LOCATE YOUR TRIBE.
Whenever you have the chance to interact with and make friends with people who have ADHD, take it! The viewpoints and experiences of several excellent TEDx speakers, bloggers, and YouTubers with ADHD are shared. Together, you can guffaw, tell tales, and confirm both the advantages and disadvantages of having an ADHD brain.

LOCATE A PLACE WHERE YOU CAN BE WHO YOU ARE.
It doesn't matter if it's on a sports field, in a music or art studio, online, or on stage. Find a location where you can be who you are without apologizing or questioning yourself, whether creative, disorganized, energetic, emotional, hyperactive, impulsive, or spontaneous.

CONCLUSION

Right, ADHD is a legitimate medical condition. The American Medical Association, American Psychiatric Association, and American Psychological Association agree that ADHD is a legitimate medical condition.

We live in an ADHD-induced society, said one business partner to one of the most renowned experts on attention deficit hyperactivity disorder.

It has long been hypothesized that because of current technological advancements and employment responsibilities, practically every single one of us finds it challenging to focus and pay attention because of the several ways we are being pushed.

At least, that is how I interpret this remark and prevailing wisdom. It seems we all have some degree of ADHD inour fast-paced environment, which requires us to perform numerous activities simultaneously. In other words, it depends more than necessary on our capacity for multitasking.

Adults with ADHD do not outgrow their disease, although many develop effective coping mechanisms. Long-term care can lessen issues at home and work, enabling patients to be more in tune with their loved ones and professional objectives.

Any person might suffer from mental health concerns at any stage of life. The best action is to speak with an expert if you or someone you love is dealing with a mental health condition. Children and adults alike might be affected by mental health concerns. If managing a mental health issue becomes difficult, one must seek professional assistance. Ignoring indicators of a mental illness, particularly in children, can have negative consequences and potentially put a person's life in danger.

The good news is that women and girls with ADHD are receiving more study and attention. Before the little girl becomes a woman, it is intended to increase awareness and put appropriate treatment plans in place so that she will not have to deal with the challenges and issues that could have been prevented with an early diagnosis.

Made in United States
North Haven, CT
16 May 2023